Praise for
Before Your Meet Your Future Husband

"Nothing derails a teenager more quickly than a misguided quest
for love—and that's why this book is essential. In a friendly, honest, relatable tone, Robin and Tricia offer truth and guidance to
help girls fall in love with their Creator before they even consider dating or marriage. The prayers and journal prompts engage
young readers and also help them self-reflect. If you want your
daughter to know the benchmark of a healthy romance and relationship, this wisdom belongs on her nightstand!"

—Kari Kampakis, bestselling author of
Love Her Well and *10 Ultimate Truths Girls Should Know*

"I love the honesty of Tricia and Robin in this book! You will be so
encouraged as they openly share their struggles and shortcomings
before marriage and how God was faithful in the midst of them.
This is a valuable read for anyone who hopes to be married or who
has teens or young adult children who hope to be married."

—Crystal Paine, *New York Times* bestselling author,
podcast host, and mom of six

"This thirty day devotional is a guiding light in an era when there
are so many lies and confusing messages about what relationships
are or should be. Robin and Tricia lead girls into preparing their
hearts and building their characters as they wait for their stories to
unfold in God's hands, not only to one day be faithful and loving
spouses but, even more so, to be the women God has set out for
them to be—women of prayer, integrity, hope, strength, and joy.
This is a beautiful book to go through alone, in a small group, or
with a mentor or mom!"

—Alyssa Bethke, author of *Satisfied*
and coauthor with Robin Jones Gunn of *Spoken For*

Before You Meet Your Future Husband

Before You Meet Your Future Husband

30 Questions to Ask Yourself and 30 Heartfelt Prayers

Robin Jones Gunn and Tricia Goyer

MULTNOMAH

Before You Meet Your Future Husband

Published in the United States by Multnomah, an imprint of Random House, a division of Penguin Random House LLC.

MULTNOMAH® and its mountain colophon are registered trademarks of Penguin Random House LLC.

Hardback ISBN 978-0-593-44477-1
Ebook ISBN 978-0-593-44478-8

The Library of Congress catalog record is available at https://lccn.loc.gov/2022020541.

Printed in Canada on acid-free paper

waterbrookmultnomah.com

9 8 7 6 5 4 3 2 1

First Edition

Book design by Diane Hobbing

SPECIAL SALES Most Multnomah books are available at special quantity discounts when purchased in bulk by corporations, organizations, and special-interest groups. Custom imprinting or excerpting can also be done to fit special needs. For information, please email specialmarketscms@penguinrandomhouse.com.

To the Dear Hearts who have a tender spot for the ways of God. May this book lead you to the One who loves you completely and has designed beautiful plans for your days.

CONTENTS

Hello, Beautiful Reader!   xi

SECTION ONE: HEART   1

Day 1. What Your Heart Needs   5

Day 2. Opening Your Heart   11

Day 3. Growing Peace in the Garden of Your Heart   17

Day 4. What Do You Treasure?   23

Day 5. Healing for a Broken Heart   27

Day 6. Forgiving from the Heart   33

Day 7. Intimacy Starts with God   41

Day 8. Guarding Your Heart   47

Day 9. Knowing God's Power = Confident Hope   53

Day 10. Desires of Your Heart   57

SECTION TWO: HEAD   63

Day 11. Hitting Refresh   67

Day 12. Trusting God with Your Future   73

Day 13. Getting Rid of Thinking Errors   79

Day 14. Calling to God in Temptation   87

Day 15. Understanding What You Need   93

Day 16. Having an Alert Mind   99

Day 17. Renewing Your Mind   105

Day 18. Being Content   111

Day 19. Time to Detox   115

Day 20. Forgiving Yourself   121

SECTION THREE: HANDS   127

Day 21. The Work of Your Hands   131

Day 22. Striving for the Ultimate Prize   137

Day 23. Holding Hands   143

Day 24. Growing in Maturity   149

Day 25. What's in Your Hands?   155

Day 26. Finding Home   163

Day 27. A Giving Hand   169

Day 28. Living Wisely   175

Day 29. Being Guided by Integrity   181

Day 30. God's Invisible Hand   185

A Final Thought   193

Discussion Questions   195

HELLO, BEAUTIFUL READER!

From Tricia

Honestly, I didn't give much thought to my future husband. Instead, I can pretty much say that all my choices about what I should do—and with whom—stemmed from a heart that longed to be loved. Born to a single mom, I didn't know my biological dad. Even though my mother told me his name once when I asked, I never met him and he wasn't involved in my life. My mom married when I was four years old, and my stepfather was distant. The longing for someone to tell me I was beautiful, worthy, and priceless created a big hole in my heart. And this gaping wound moved up to my head, where it echoed, *I need someone to love me! I need a boyfriend!* (I bet you can imagine that didn't lead anywhere good, right?)

My longing to be loved, and my craving for a boyfriend, led me to heartache. I would find someone I thought was wonderful, then be crushed when he didn't like me. Of course, this didn't help my already-hurting heart. I felt more unloved and more unworthy.

Finally the day came when someone I was attracted to was interested in me. Not only was he interested in me, but he was also amazing: tall with blond hair and crystal-blue eyes. He was three years older than I was. I couldn't believe my luck. When he asked me to be his girlfriend, our relationship quickly became physical. My heart soared when we were together, and my mind claimed, *This is forever! Finally I've found what I've been looking for!*

Then, months later, he moved away. To say I was crushed is an understatement. I was truly broken: in my heart, head, and body.

I wish I could say that at this point I took a step back and decided to do things differently. But again my heart ruled, roping in my mind and body. I found it easy to date guys and give my whole self away in my search for "love." Yet those choices often led to more pain. Eventually I found myself pregnant.

Still in high school, I took what I thought was the easy way out, choosing abortion. That decision brought more emptiness, shame, and heartache. I deeply regretted that choice moments after I went through with it.

Now I saw myself as wholly unworthy. My future looked dark, with no hope, no light. Still seeking love in all the wrong ways, I soon found myself in the same situation: pregnant and abandoned by my boyfriend. Yet this time, I made a different choice: I decided to have my baby.

I clearly remember the day when I was six months pregnant and realized what a pain-filled path my empty heart had led me on. That day I prayed, "God, I have screwed up big time. If You can do anything with my life, please do."

Light, love, and hope flooded in, and I've never been the same! Jesus took my broken, empty, hurting heart and filled it with Himself. He also gave me a desire to do things differently—correctly.

That's when I started praying for my future husband. I also started asking God to change me, to prepare me for him.

God in His mercy quickly answered my prayers. Two weeks after my son Cory was born, I started to date John Goyer, my pastor's son. As I'm writing this, we've been married thirty-two years!

Needless to say, I wish I would have given more thought to my future husband from the start. That's why I wanted to write this book with my longtime friend Robin. First, to help you recognize how our desires, thoughts, and actions affect everything. And second, because I want you to understand what I didn't know for many years: You are loved and worthy, and God has good plans for your life. Those plans may include finding your future husband, or He may lead you on another path. But I hope your life's journey will be one of falling deeper in love with the Creator of your soul.

If you couldn't quite relate to my experience, maybe you'll see yourself in Robin—a girl who grew up in a family that went to church. Her parents were protective of her, paying attention to what she did and whom she hung out with.

When you read her story next, you'll notice that we both had the same desires: to be wanted and loved. Doesn't every young woman feel that way?

From Robin

As a young woman, I often felt driven by the same longings Tricia described. I wanted to be desired, loved, and cherished—or at least noticed.

Being a middle child probably added to my need for attention. Having a matter-of-fact, efficient mom and a kind but reserved dad may have added to my longing for affection. I dreamed of being sought by a guy who thought I was lovely.

Those feelings stayed hidden in my early teen years because of the conservative Christian circles in which our family orbited. For my sister and me, makeup, music, magazines, and, of course, dating were restricted. Our mom sewed most of our modest clothing, including our bathing suits. I have a picture of me at Newport Beach in a lime-green polka-dot creation of hers. Oh, and it had ruffles. Cute for a four-year-old, maybe. I was fifteen. Also, I didn't have a driver's license until I was eighteen.

None of those social hindrances stopped me from "falling in love" repeatedly before I turned twenty-two. I met my first "true love" at church camp when I was fourteen. He was so cute. I was a Christian; he was a Christian. It was perfect.

On the last night of camp, he walked me to the closing campfire and sat next to me. Our shoulders brushed, and my heart felt like it had been lit on fire. I was sure he was "the one." We became pen pals after camp, and for my birthday he sent me a gold ID bracelet. Our long-distance, innocent "love" endured our freshman year of high school. Then the frequency of our sweet, handwritten letters slowed, and our "true love" drifted away on a cloud.

My desire to have a real, day-to-day boyfriend became a constant thought. I dreamed about what it would be like to have a guy hold my hand, kiss me, and smile at me. I found ways to work around my parents' socializing restrictions by going on church outreach trips and flirting with the cutest guy on the bus. I made sure my partner for class projects was my current crush. Youth group events and camps were gold mines in my relentless hunt for a boyfriend.

The curious factor in my quest to find love was that I had a deep respect for God. I wanted His blessing. I wanted to serve Him and follow His Word. I honestly tried to do what was right—most of the time. I think, in a way, I wanted to make Him proud of me. I didn't understand that wasn't what my heavenly Father wanted from our relationship.

My focus was constantly on myself. How could I love myself more, accept my uniqueness, and be more attractive? Where did I need to go and what did I need to do to find "the one"? Surely God wanted me to be happy, and marrying someday would make me happy, wouldn't it?

Over the next eight years, I experienced a variety of relationships with a lot of young men. Some friendships were the true brother-and-sister-in-Christ type, and the fellowship remains. Some relationships were destructive, even though we both thought of ourselves as Christians. One was manipulative and abusive, but I was young and too naive to see it at the time. I messed up one relationship because I never cared for him as much as he cared for me and I waited too long to tell him. I liked the attention too much.

At the end of my sophomore year at a Christian college, I became engaged. We had been together for a year, and when he graduated, he bought me a ring. I loved him—meaning that I didn't want the pace of our complex relationship to change. We had worked so hard to get to where we were. Surely all those heart-to-heart talks and all the laughter and tears meant something.

Six months into our engagement, with my wedding dress hanging in the closet and the invitations on order at the printer's, he told me he didn't love me and could never marry me. Oh, and he thought it was only right to tell me he had been with his previous girlfriend the night before, so there was that.

That was the day I began to deconstruct my concept of love and what it meant to find "the one."

I think that was also when I started to write this book. I didn't know then that it would turn into a book, nor had it entered my mind that one day I would become an author. All I knew was that my heart and head had wandered for years in a cultural and self-induced fairy tale. What was true love? What example could I learn from? Would I ever be able to trust another man and commit to another relationship? Would any man ever love me completely?

All the answers led me back to Christ. His love for me was like an ancient secret hidden in plain sight. All those years, I had been trying to fall in love with the right guy, yet True Love was right there. Jesus waited so patiently for me to turn my heart fully to Him and to fall in love with Him.

When I gave my life to Him, He opened His arms to me as His bride. He promised to always be with me and be the source of all my joy and contentment. The foundation for all love is from Him, through Him, and because of Him.

As I began to understand how much Jesus wanted me, all the other pieces of my life shifted into place. I saw that God would fulfill His purpose for me as I continued to live in a committed relationship with Him. If a spouse was part of His faultless purpose, God wouldn't withhold that relationship from me. He would accomplish His beautiful design in His way and in His time. If not, then I would still spend my life fully being who I was created to be. No anxiety. No regrets. Only hope and confidence in all the ways the Holy Spirit was at work in me.

I wrote in my journal, "I wish I would have understood the real source of love earlier. How can I help girls who are frantic to find love the way I was?"

Soon after I wrote that, I went on a youth group outing as a leader and told the young teen girls what it was like to fall in love with Jesus. I told them that He was their everything and that they would be changed inside if they feasted on His love letter to them, the Bible. I told them how lavishly He loved them.

Now here I am, telling you the same truth. God's love for you is eternal. He is The One for you. He is your true First Love.

When I met the man who has now been my husband for decades, we didn't think much about each other at first. But when we connected again two years later, everything was different. During that time, both of us had recalibrated our focus. I knew that I didn't need a man to save me. Jesus already had done that.

On our first real date, that guy—the one who would become my husband—didn't tell me that I was cute or had a nice smile or that he wanted to kiss me. (All that came later.) Instead, unlike any other guy I'd dated, he told me that he loved God and that his heavenly Father would always have first place in his life. I think that was the moment I started to fall in love with him. For several years I'd been writing letters to my future husband, and those were the same words I'd been writing to some mysterious man I hadn't met yet. We quickly saw that our hearts and minds were on parallel paths. Marriage would be a continuation of our walk with the Lord as we joined together to finish the journey God had put each of us on.

How will your story unfold? Will you get married one day? Will you meet a man traveling down a parallel path, join hearts and lives, and keep on going together?

I don't know. Your future is a beautiful mystery.

Tricia and I hope this book will be an encouragement as you journey on into that beautiful mystery. We wanted to share our personal stories so that they might help focus your thinking and prepare your heart before you meet your future husband.

Above all, our prayer is that you will fall in love with Jesus. You have been chosen by the Prince of Peace to be His bride now and forever. Before you meet your eternal Husband in heaven, may this book draw you closer to His heart.

Your Bridegroom, Jesus, loves you more than you will ever know.

Section ONE

HEART

From Robin

Tricia and I had lots of ideas on how to organize the thoughts we wanted to share with you in this book. Our conclusion was to create three sections: Heart, Head, and Hands.

We wanted to start with the heart because, for better or for worse, the heart is where we hold on to and examine our feelings. Love, in its simplest form, usually starts with a feeling. The Bible talks about the heart in more than six hundred places, including Matthew 22:37, where we are told, "Love the Lord your God with all your heart" (NIV).

The heart is the dwelling place of all love. It's also our personal treasure chest, where we keep what we value. That's why Proverbs 4:23 says, "Above all else, guard your heart, for everything you do flows from it" (NIV).

Did you catch that?

It doesn't say that a few things are inspired by your heart. It says that *everything* is. It also doesn't say, "Don't pay attention to what your heart is telling you."

No. Everything flows from the heart—it's the wellspring of your whole life. That's why we must pay close attention to what we take in or hold on to and guard our hearts above all else.

When a root of bitterness takes hold in a broken heart, it soon grows into a toxic vine that not only lashes out at others but also entangles and hinders us. Before you meet your future husband, you'll want to make sure you've ripped out all roots of bitterness and planted seeds of hope and peace in freshly turned soil. Good things grow alongside hope and peace in a cleaned-up heart. It's the ideal environment for love to grow.

From Tricia

When I was growing up, I heard a lot about "following your heart" and not very much about "guarding your heart." I didn't see my heart as something to protect. Instead, I believed that I needed to figure out how to fill the emptiness I had inside. I wish someone back then would have told me how precious my heart is. I wish I had known how to tend it well. That's what Robin and I hope to help you discover in the following section.

All the wrong decisions I made as a young woman started with my trying to find a guy to fill my heart. That led to a lot of brokenness. I'm so thankful God gave me a new heart to replace the broken pieces that resulted from bad decisions. (I'll tell you more about that concept later in the book.)

Whether or not you marry someday, guarding your heart will protect you from a lot of pain.

Now let's ponder what's in our hearts and what adjustments we might need to make to plant a beautiful garden there.

DAY 1

WHAT YOUR HEART NEEDS

Tricia

Take delight in the Lord,
  and he will give you your heart's desires.

Psalm 37:4

When I was seven years old, I wanted a Barbie paper doll book with cute two-dimensional clothes to punch out. I desperately wanted it, so I prayed. I had heard a lot of Bible stories, and I knew, if God could heal a blind man, He could make a paper doll book appear. I told God that He could drop the book in my closet and I'd keep it just between Him and me.

I prayed as long and hard as a second grader could. But the next day, when I opened the closet door, the paper doll book wasn't there. How could that be? Wasn't God supposed to answer my prayers?

A few weeks later, my birthday arrived. Guess what I received? Yes, the paper doll book, among other things.

From that experience, I learned a lot about God and myself. Even though my thought process and prayers were immature, I knew I could turn to God with the desires of my heart. But I learned that sometimes prayers aren't answered in the ways we want. As I grew older, I realized I didn't need to bargain with God or expect Him to be some sort of magician who makes whatever I want appear (no, not even in my closet). Instead, it's okay just to share what's on my heart.

Father God knows the desires of our hearts, and He will handle those desires in tender ways. Sometimes He will ask us to wait, knowing the time isn't right. Other times He will turn our hearts to different desires.

Pause and consider what you truly desire in terms of your future husband. Make a list. Then look at that list and pray about those desires.

Is it hard to trust God with your desires? The more you delight yourself in the Lord, the more you'll understand how good God's heart is toward you. As you delight in Him, your trust in Him will grow. As you pray, you'll see that His answers are for good, even if they are different from what you wanted.

God cares about your desires, but mostly He cares about you. He knows when—or if—your future husband will come and how that person will be the man you truly need, someone your heart will also desire.

What desires of your heart do you need to turn over entirely to God, especially concerning your future husband?

Father God,

You know the desires of my heart. Could You help me trust You with those desires? I know that what I want now might not be what's best for me. So guide me to delight in You. Enable me to trust that You know the perfect gift of a future husband for me and that You will bring him to me at the ideal time. Help me trust that You will give me what I desire or provide me with someone or something better.

I ask this in the name of Your Son, Jesus. Amen.

DAY 2

OPENING YOUR HEART

Robin

> If you openly declare that Jesus is Lord and believe in
> your heart that God raised him from the dead, you will
> be saved.
>
> *Romans 10:9*

Human nature yearns to know and to be known. This heart-to-heart closeness infuses a marriage with a beautiful, one-of-a-kind intimacy and love. If we want to get to know someone, we have to be willing to open up to them, to receive them completely. We need to spend time with them and let them get to know us at the same level that we're coming to know them.

God made it possible for us to experience the same heart-to-heart closeness with Him through His Son. Think of it! The Creator of this universe wants an intimate relationship with you. He is waiting for you to come to Him. It starts when you open your heart and receive the gift of His love through Jesus.

A few months ago, I was at a wedding held in a beautiful chapel on a bluff above the Pacific Ocean. It was a gorgeous day. The chapel's tall glass windows provided extraordinary views of the sea for miles. The flowers, the music, and the sunshine all filled the space with the sense that we were part of a sacred moment.

The minister entered and took his place. The groom followed with a look of patient expectation. The congregation rose and watched as the radiant bride came down the aisle to join her groom. I couldn't hold back the silent tears. It was all so beautiful. I knew their love story well. I had prayed for her and for him for years. They were finally becoming man and wife.

Their defining moment at the altar when she said "I do" took my breath away. I felt as if I was witnessing an earthly representation of the sacred union that happens between Christ Jesus and us when we open our hearts to Him. God has sent an invitation to each of us to come to "the wedding feast of the Lamb" (Revelation 19:7). He even calls us "the bride" in the Bible, and Jesus is called "the bridegroom."

Picture yourself as a glowing, desired bride. You are walking down the aisle. Your heavenly Father stands before you. Next to Him stands Jesus, who has paid the ultimate price to make this union possible.

God turns to His only, beloved Son and says, "Jesus, do You take this woman to be Your bride and love her forever?" Looking you in the eye with a heart overflowing with pure love, Jesus says, "I do."

Now God turns to you. "My daughter, do you take Jesus to be your bridegroom to love forever?"

And you say . . .

What do you say? How would you respond? At such a moment, face-to-face and heart-to-heart with the Prince of Peace, would you say, "Umm, I don't know. Let me think about it"? Would you say, "I want to try out some other love interests first, and then maybe I'll come back to You later"?

Or would you open your heart and say, "I do"? Would you let the intimacy and the never-ending love relationship begin with the One who will never leave you and will always love you?

If you haven't yet said "I do" to Jesus the Bridegroom, are you ready to receive Him as your Lord and Savior right now? If you have already said "I do" to the Lord, in what ways are you becoming closer in your relationship with Him?

Heavenly Father,

Thank You for loving me unconditionally and for inviting me into Your family. Forgive me for all the wrong I've done. I want to receive the gift of Your love through Jesus. I open my heart to Him now and promise to spend the rest of my life growing in love with Him. I want to be with Jesus every moment, for better or worse, for richer or poorer, in sickness and in health. Best of all, I know that I will be with Him forever.

I pray this in the name that is now written on my heart. Amen.

DAY 3

GROWING PEACE IN THE GARDEN OF YOUR HEART

Tricia

May the LORD bless you
and protect you.
May the LORD smile on you
and be gracious to you.
May the LORD show you his favor
and give you his peace.

Numbers 6:24–26

Have you ever visited the house of a grandparent, aunt, or uncle, and they've called out as you left, "Be safe and drive carefully"? Of course, we plan to be safe. We have no plans to drive recklessly. These common phrases aren't directions to follow. Instead, they can be considered blessings. Our loved ones want us to be safe, and their words are a send-off with hope for good things.

Similarly, in the Bible, God's priests prayed blessings over His people. First, the priests taught God's children about His truth and laws. And then, when the people went on their way, the priests offered a blessing as a holy send-off, like the one on the previous page.

The priests prayed for God's protection over the people, but more than that, the priests wanted the people to understand God's love and favor. It's only when we embrace the love and approval of God that peace comes.

Just as plants need good soil, water, and sun to grow, peace grows in our hearts when we understand how much God loves us. Peace comes when we feel blessed and protected. Peace comes when we know that God unconditionally offers us grace and forgiveness. These things feed our souls and help peace grow.

Whenever you feel worried that your future husband will never come or that he won't be everything you hoped for when he does come, you can turn to God. Peace comes when we understand God's smile on us and our lives.

Yet, to understand God's smile, we have to look up. We have to lift our eyes from the troubles around us and turn to Him. God doesn't just like us—He adores us. Knowing that the God of the universe looks on us with such tenderness should fill us with peace in all things.

How can you remind yourself to look to God and seek His peace instead of letting the worries of this world claim your attention?

Father God,

    I pray that You will bless me and protect me. I pray that You will smile on me and be gracious to me. I pray that You will show me Your favor and give me Your peace. I pray that I will learn to lift my eyes daily to You and truly understand Your love for me. Help me, Lord, not to be distracted by the worries of this world but instead to put my trust in You.

    I pray the same for my future husband, and I ask all this in the name of Your Son, Jesus. Amen.

Relax, everything's going to be all right; rest, everything's coming together; open your hearts, love is on the way!

—JUDE 2, MSG

DAY 4

WHAT DO YOU TREASURE?

Robin

Mary treasured up all these things, pondering them in
her heart.

Luke 2:19, ESV

I loved watching our daughter when she was young, how she val-
ued certain qualities such as honesty, kindness, patience, and trust
in God. Those gems maintained their assigned value during her
teens and twenties as she dated. I found it beautiful to watch her
hold fast to what she treasured, even when so many of her friends
were shifting their values and changing their goals. She knew what
qualities mattered most in a future husband, and she stored the same
traits in her own heart.

Many of those prized attributes developed in her life as she
prayerfully went through different relationships. I cried with her
over breakups and laughed over ridiculous first dates that were dead

ends. (One guy owned a pet raccoon that lived in the house and walked on its back legs across the living room!) She continued to treasure her values and didn't trade any of them for temporary relationships that would turn to dust. As the years went on, she grew in patience and peace as she trusted God to bring the right man into her life at the right time.

One night she called to tell me about a guy she was thinking about meeting for coffee. They hadn't met face-to-face yet, but she was willing to take a chance because there was just something about him. She had checked out his social media and had a good feeling about him.

I asked his name because, of course, I wanted to check him out too.

"You can marry him," I said when I heard his name.

"Marry him! I haven't even met him yet."

I couldn't stop smiling as I told her, "His mom was my college roommate, and we went to the same church when we were in high school. You have to at least meet him."

They met and talked for hours. He walked her to her front door, placed his hand on her shoulder, and said, "May I pray for you?" She was smitten.

Their wedding was a joyful celebration as well as a sweet reunion of family and friends who hadn't seen one another for years. Our daughter and her groom were patient and trusted God's timing and His leading, all the while holding on to what they treasured. They had prayed for each other for years before they met. His mom had prayed for her future daughter-in-law. I had prayed for my future son-in-law. Many prayers were answered on their wedding day. I still smile when I think about how God was orchestrating their love story long before they were even born.

What are the traits you treasure most in a future husband, and how are you trusting God to develop those golden traits in your life right now?

Father God,

I want to trust You. Teach me how to do that completely. Help me see the big picture and believe that You have a plan for my life that is better than I could ever imagine. Show me the things in life that are true treasures. Teach me how to rid the treasure chest of my heart of all the things I've stored there that are not of value in Your kingdom. Fill my heart and my life with true treasure.

In Jesus's name, amen.

DAY 5

HEALING FOR A BROKEN HEART

Tricia

> I will give you a new heart, and I will put a new spirit
> in you. I will take out your stony, stubborn heart and
> give you a tender, responsive heart.
>
> *Ezekiel 36:26*

I wonder how many young women believe that their first boyfriend is "the one," like I did. Buying into the instant-romance story lines of the movies I watched, I thought I'd found the guy who was right for me. Yet even if my first boyfriend hadn't moved away, I know now that our relationship wouldn't have lasted. We had no foundation on which to build a relationship or a life together. My broken heart came from placing my hope in the wrong place and the wrong person—and from not preparing for the right person.

I wish I could say that I learned from my error of "falling in love" fast. Instead, I made the same mistake a few more times until it seemed my broken heart was irreparable. As I shared at the start of this book, by the time I was seventeen—and pregnant—despair overwhelmed me.

When I finally made the decision to trust God, I pictured all the broken pieces of my heart and envisioned myself daring to lift them to Him. "God, if You can do anything with this . . ." I prayed.

The most beautiful thing happened next. God didn't glue together the broken pieces. He gave me a new heart. It's not that the ache stopped completely, but I did feel the transformation deep inside. Where despair once reigned, hope replaced it. I began to believe that God had a good purpose for me. And I no longer desperately needed a boyfriend. Then, as I became content in God's love, I attracted the type of person who also loved God. John told me that my love for God was what drew him to me, and I'm glad!

Healing happens when we turn our broken hearts over to God. He longs to give us new hearts. He also longs to bring healing, which allows us to hope. It's a gift that will change everything from the inside out.

What has broken your heart, and what would it look like for you to turn the pieces over to God today?

Father God,

The truth is that my heart has been broken as I've looked to others for the wrong type of love. I know that human relationships can never give me the kind of love I desire. So today, Lord, I give You my broken heart. I pray You will provide me with a new heart in return. I know that only with You in the center of my heart can I achieve healthy relationships. Re-create me from the inside out as only You can.

I ask this in the name of Your Son, Jesus. Amen.

There is no charm equal to tenderness of heart.

—JANE AUSTEN, *Emma*

Day 6

Forgiving from the Heart

Robin

When you are praying, first forgive anyone you are
holding a grudge against, so that your Father in heaven
will forgive you your sins too.

Mark 11:25, TLB

I have yet to meet someone who hasn't been hurt deeply. Each
wound that friends have told me about is different, but each hits at
the heart level. For many, the invisible arrows became embedded in
their hearts.

That's how it was in my heart for many years. I tried not to
"bleed" all over the place when a certain painful topic came up. I
made jokes about the hurt. I brushed off the actions of the person
who had wounded me so deeply. Then I would conclude with,
"But I've forgiven him."

One day as I talked with a couple of friends, one of them called me out on my tidy summary. "No, you haven't."

"Yes, I have. Really. It's in the past. I've forgiven him."

"You may have said in your head that you've forgiven him," my friend said, "but the injury didn't happen in your head. It happened in your heart. You must choose to forgive from the heart if you want to be free."

As the three of us talked, my defenses lowered. My friend was right. I wasn't free. I was holding a grudge. We prayed together and my tears flowed. In that moment, I had moved out of my head and all the way into the deep place in my heart where the attack had happened and the pain had settled. I told God that I wanted to be free and that I chose, from my heart, to release that person from the offense I'd held against him. It was different from the times in the past when I thought I was forgiving him. This time as I prayed, I felt the hurt, and I also felt as if the arrow was removed. God's authority, His power, released me from the hurt and released the other person from the wrong he had done to me.

I said "Amen" and looked at my friend with a smile. I felt released and ready to completely heal from the past. He told me that if the enemy came back and tried to get me to pick up the arrow and stick it back into the wound, I needed to remember this moment and the way we had just prayed.

"You might have to pray this way—from the heart—a number of times before the wound heals completely," he said. "That's okay. It's good work. Do it again. Forgiveness can be a process. I'm just glad that when God says we're forgiven, He means it. It's gone, right then and there."

We all have been hurt deeply. But none of us needs to hold on to that hurt and continue to relive the pain. The only way for you to be free is by forgiving. Fresh, happy, and healthy relationships have room to grow in vibrant ways once all the toxic remnants of old hurts have been removed. Otherwise, you're planting new sprouts in poisoned soil. How can those green shoots thrive?

Get your heart ready to welcome new relationships. Take the important first step—go to the heart level and choose to forgive. You'll be amazed at how much freedom and peace you'll feel.

Who do you need to forgive from the heart right now?

Father God,

You offer complete forgiveness to me. Thank You, God. I'm so grateful. I confess to You that it's difficult for me to want to go back to the heart level of my hurt and choose to forgive that person. Give me the power and the willingness to forgive. Set me free. Release the person who hurt me too. I can't do this without You, Lord. But I see now that I can never have deep peace and freedom until I do this.

Please help me, Lord. Amen.

Forgiveness is the key
that unlocks the door of
resentment and the handcuffs
of hatred. It is a power that
breaks the chains of bitterness
and the shackles of selfishness.
What a liberation it is when
you can forgive.

—CORRIE TEN BOOM, *Jesus Is Victor*

DAY 7

INTIMACY STARTS WITH GOD

Tricia

> Everything that goes into a life of pleasing God has
> been miraculously given to us by getting to know,
> personally and intimately, the One who invited us to
> God.
>
> *2 Peter 1:3, MSG*

In most songs and movies, "love" is shown through physical intimacy. Two people gaze into each other's eyes, have a conversation,
and then sleep together. Yet this is far from true intimacy. One way
to break down the word is to read it this way: *into-me-see*. Intimacy
is allowing someone to know the deepest parts of you.

It's only natural to hide our true selves from God and others.
What if we allow someone to see the real us but they don't like
what they see?

The first step to intimacy with others is seeing ourselves as God sees us. When we see ourselves as God does, we too can say, "I praise you, for I am fearfully and wonderfully made" (Psalm 139:14, ESV). We have to trust that God created us to fulfill His good plans to benefit ourselves, the world, and our future families. When we see ourselves as God sees us, we are more willing to allow others to see our true selves too. And if one day God brings into your life a husband, he will appreciate who you are. He won't want you to change to make him happy. To be truly loved by someone in this way brings a unique peace. But even before that, being loved by God in this way can make your heart sing!

Today the Lord can be your strength and your song, and He can give you victory over every part of your life, including your struggles with true intimacy. When you are empty, any type of love will do, including "love" that isn't love at all. Accepting Jesus's love—and getting to know Him intimately—fills you up. You won't need false love to fill the void.

To prepare yourself for intimacy with your future husband, open your heart to intimacy with Jesus. Allowing Jesus to see the deepest parts of you is the first step to letting your future husband genuinely know you too.

How can intimacy with Jesus prepare your heart for intimacy with your future husband?

Father God,

I admit that the idea of intimacy (into-me-see) is scary. I'm afraid that when others see the true me, they won't like what they see. I often want to change to fit the role I believe others expect of me. Yet I know my relationships will bring only hurt and not joy when I do this. Instead, Lord, help me grow in intimacy with Jesus. Help me genuinely know how much You love and adore me. When doubts come, I pray that You will bring peace. Help me grow in intimacy with You so my heart will be prepared to do the same with my future husband.

I thank You, Lord, that You can give me victory in this area. I ask this in the name of Your Son, Jesus. Amen.

DAY 8

GUARDING YOUR HEART

Robin

> Guard your heart above all else,
> for it determines the course of your life.
>
> *Proverbs 4:23*

Imagine going to view a house you are interested in renting and finding that the lock on the front door is missing. Inside is a smelly mess with broken appliances, and one of the bedrooms is painted black. The screen door to the backyard has been sliced to tatters, and you watch as several cats and a dog come and go, scrounging around the overturned trash can. Who would say yes to living in such a place?

Actually, my husband and I did when we lived in Hawaii.

Before we moved in, though, the inside was gutted and sanitized. The screens and front door were replaced. The rooms were painted. Before the new flooring went in, we wrote verses on the cleaned cement. Each room was prayed over. I wrote *Hale Maluhia* on the floor in the center of the house. It's Hawaiian for "house of peace."

We left the windows open during the renovations to let the fragrant tropical trade winds flow through the house. It felt like we were watching the space come back to life after being stifled and mistreated for years.

The day after we moved in, a friend stopped by with a housewarming bouquet. She hadn't seen the disastrous "before" version. The first thing she said was, "It's so peaceful. I can't believe you found a place this nice. Housing on this part of Maui is scarce." I let her know how far the little house had come and how much love had gone into the cleansing and renovation. She couldn't believe the changes.

That night, my husband closed and locked the doors before we went to bed. I felt safe. Protected and tranquil in our new haven.

Our hearts can become tranquil havens too. They need to be cleansed. They need God's Word to be written on the foundation. And they need to be protected.

Imagine how terrible it would have been to go to all the work of renovating our little house and then not fix the torn screens or replace the front door. I'm sure all the cats in the neighborhood would have returned and treated the floors as a kitty litter box again.

Think of all the times you've asked God to forgive you and cleanse your heart. The refreshing change will be short-lived unless you guard your heart. You must be the one who puts doors, locks, and screens in place to keep all the bad stuff outside. You do that by turning off or turning away from anything that fills your heart with images, words, or other messages that don't honor God.

The Holy Spirit longs to cleanse our hearts. He wants to renovate the mess and bring us peace. We must guard our hearts above all else, as Proverbs 4:23 says, because our hearts really do determine the course of our lives.

Think about what you watch, read, and listen to. How much of it is wholesome and God-honoring, and how much of it has placed images, thoughts, and feelings in your heart that are beginning to stink?

Father God,

I want the Holy Spirit to renovate my heart. I want to have a clean heart before You. Please cleanse me once again, Lord, and teach me how to guard my heart. Show me clearly the things You want me to turn away from, and give me the courage to do so, even if I'm the only one.

I ask this in the name of Your Son, Jesus. Amen.

DAY 9

KNOWING GOD'S POWER = CONFIDENT HOPE

Tricia

I pray that your hearts will be flooded with light so
that you can understand the confident hope he has
given to those he called—his holy people who are his
rich and glorious inheritance.

I also pray that you will understand the incredible
greatness of God's power for us who believe him. This
is the same mighty power that raised Christ from the
dead and seated him in the place of honor at God's
right hand in the heavenly realms.

Ephesians 1:18–20

Years ago, my husband and I traveled to Niagara Falls only to find
less than one-third of the usual volume going over the waterfall.

The falls are a source of hydropower, and because of a blackout in New York City, water had been diverted to make more power. Even though the water flow was greatly reduced, the falls still were impressive.

As I stood at the edge of the mighty waterfall, I couldn't imagine how spectacular it must be at full capacity. Unfortunately, John and I had to travel home before the energy crisis was over, so we never saw the full force of the falls.

Yet I was reminded of how little I understand God's power. I'm impressed when I pray a small prayer and see it answered. How much greater would my hope be if I dared to pray big prayers and waited to see God work?

The same mighty power that raised Jesus from the dead is available to us, God's children. When we doubt that God can bring us someone we will truly love, we forget God's power. When we doubt that God can bring us someone who will love us unconditionally in return, we forget God's power. When we have a hard time believing that God has good plans for us—husband or no husband—we forget God's power. Just as I couldn't imagine the full force of Niagara Falls, I often have a hard time picturing the beautiful future God has for me. Do you feel the same?

The more we courageously trust God, the more His light floods our hearts. The more light, the more hope we have—confident hope. God's power is always available, yet hope gives us the confidence to access it. If, as His daughter, you boldly access God's power, you'll be impressed at how He answers you. Dare to hope, and you'll be inspired to hope even more!

What is one fear concerning your future husband that you can hand over to your powerful God, allowing Him to fill your heart with hope instead?

Father God,

You know that sometimes I'm afraid to hope. So I pray that my heart will be flooded with light, enabling me to experience confident hope in You. Help me know that I'm called by You. Fill my heart with joy because You consider me Your daughter. Fill me with gratitude that You have a glorious inheritance prepared for me.

Help me, Lord, to understand the incredible greatness of Your power that is available when I dare to believe You. Help me also know that the power available to me is the same mighty power that raised Your Son, Jesus Christ, from the dead and seated Him in the place of honor at Your right hand in the heavenly realms.

May Your power give me confidence today for myself and my future. I ask this in the name of Your Son, Jesus. Amen.

DAY 10

DESIRES OF YOUR HEART

Robin

> May He give you what your heart desires
> and fulfill your whole purpose.
>
> *Psalm 20:4, HCSB*

One of the best letters I ever received came from a woman in her forties who heard me speak at a conference. It was short and sweet: "You were right. God does know me by heart."

A few months later, she sent a picture of herself leading a women's group. She looked radiant, and all her email said was, "You were right. God did have a bigger purpose for my life." The third letter came almost a year later. It was an invitation to her wedding. She added a note: "You were right. God does give us the desires of our hearts. Why did it take me so long to believe that?"

When a woman truly believes that God loves her and knows everything about her—including the desires of her heart—it changes

her from the inside out. When she asks God to reveal His purpose
for her life, amazing things begin to happen.

Pause right now and think about those hidden hopes and wishes
that you've kept in the corner of your heart. If you're a list maker,
write them down. If you prefer to sift through the options mentally, give yourself time and space to ponder deeply.

I've been writing down my hopes and wishes every year since I
was a teenager. It has become a sacred time between God and me. I
set aside time on a quiet day early in the new year.

First I surrender all my assumptions and expectations to the Lord
and ask Him to fulfill His whole purpose for me. I don't want to miss
out on anything He created me to do or be.

Then I write in my journal. Sometimes it comes out sounding
like a love letter to Jesus because I get overwhelmed when I see all
the wonderful things He has done over the years. As I write, I pay
attention to the desires that begin to surface in my heart, and I write
them down. Even the ones that seem silly. I find it's valuable to record each thought when it comes.

Going back and reading those lists and love letters, I'm always
amazed to see the prayers and purposes that God fulfilled as well as
the many whims that simply fluttered away. Things that seemed so
important at one time no longer stir my heart when I read them. I
know it's because God has led me into something else that will fulfill my whole purpose.

Why don't you give it a try? First, surrender everything and everyone in your life and ask God to fulfill His purpose for you. His
Spirit then has freedom to move around in your heart and mind. I
believe this is the beautiful way that our loving Lord opens the
channels through which He will give you the desires of your heart.
You become intimately connected with Him, and your desires become one with His desires.

What changes can you make to show that you have surrendered your desires and expectations to Christ and asked Him to fulfill His purpose for you?

Creator of the Universe,

You know all things. You know how many hairs are on my head. You saw me before I was even born. You know the desires of my heart. I surrender everything in my life to You and ask that You bless me and open the pathways that will lead me to Your purpose for my life.

You created me for a beautiful purpose. I believe that, and I ask that You fulfill Your purpose for me. I now believe that Your desires are becoming my true desires. Continue to refine my whims and wishes, and according to Your great love for me, please give me the true desires of my heart.

I ask this in the name of Your Son. Amen.

Where there is great love there are always miracles.

—WILLA CATHER,
Death Comes for the Archbishop

Section TWO

HEAD

From Robin

"What are you thinking?" How many times have you asked someone that question, and how many times has someone asked you? We called this section "Head" because once your heart is settled, the next area to focus on is your thoughts.

Changes in our lives begin with realigning our thoughts. Romans 12:2 describes this process as being "transformed by the renewing of your mind" (NIV). We're told that the result of this renewal is that we then can know God's will. In a world filled with confusion, this is a gift. We can know what God has orchestrated for us. Through the renewing of our minds, we can and will be changed.

You might know that Tricia and I co-authored another book titled *Praying for Your Future Husband*. We heard from some of its readers that when they were young, before reading our book, they fixated on an image of what their future husband was supposed to be like. They held on to those expectations, and even as adults, they would only consider men who looked a certain way, had a particular career, or shared a specific interest.

Upon reading our book, they were prompted to pray for their future husband, and as they did, their thinking took a different route. Their long list of expectations was exchanged for the life-giving freedom of focusing only on what really matters for eternity. You'll be surprised at the clarity that comes when you let go of thinking errors and lies.

From Tricia

Beginning in the sixth grade, I was obsessed with guys. I always had a crush on one or more: Jason, Simon, and Keith, to name a few. Yes, I was the one who was always scribbling their names in my notebooks. Then I would try out how their last names looked with my first name.

Only later did I figure out that I serve whatever I think about most. When I turned my heart over to God, I turned my thoughts over to Him too. Then, with a change of thoughts, I started to act differently. (We'll talk about that in the next section.)

After you focus on opening your heart to God, He often will work on your mind next. Take your time as you go through this section. We hope you'll ponder the questions and write down your thoughts.

Let the transformation begin!

DAY 11

HITTING REFRESH

Robin

> We break down every thought and proud thing that
> puts itself up against the wisdom of God. We take hold
> of every thought and make it obey Christ.
>
> *2 Corinthians 10:5, NLV*

An elderly relative handed me his battered phone. "What's wrong with this?" he asked. "I can't get it to do what I want." I found the problem quickly. He had opened hundreds of files and apps and never closed any of them. He had also opened links in emails that clogged his phone with spam, and he had never deleted any texts or voicemails. All that data was running in the background and draining the real power of his phone. Within a few minutes, I'd cleared it, and his cellphone was refreshed and ready to go.

Try the same process with your thoughts. What unrealistic data is still running in the background of your thoughts? What messages have you saved that should have been deleted long ago? What kind of spam has infiltrated your mind? Perhaps your imagination has held on to an impression of what romance should look like from a movie you loved as a child, but nothing in real life has measured up. Maybe you took to heart painful words from a broken relationship. You're still running those discouraging messages in the background and believing lies. To move forward, you need to swipe clear your imagination and hit refresh so that you can be ready for what comes next.

One of the many amazing things about our Father God is that He is the Author and Finisher of our faith. He can write your love story in ways that are far more creative, mysterious, hilarious, and beautiful than anything you could dream up.

But you must let Him do the writing.

Go ahead. Start now by deleting everything in the background of your thoughts that doesn't align with what God has for you. How do you know which thoughts are from Him and which are the rogue ones that sneaked in there and set up an entire camp? Simple. You ask Him. I've suggested a prayer at the end of this reading that will help you start the process.

No shame here. Just a fresh start. Once your thoughts are cleared and refreshed, you'll have mental and emotional space to fill up with right thinking and aligned emotions.

What thoughts about yourself and/or your future husband have you held on to that God is now asking you to let go of?

Father God,

You know everything about me. Please show me the thoughts I've held on to that aren't true and aren't part of the story You want to write in my life. I surrender to You all the wrong and unnecessary thoughts taking up space in my mind. Release me from any lies that have poisoned my thoughts.

Lord, I want You to be the Author of my love story. I want my ideas to be honoring to You. Protect me from the enemy, who plots evil against me because I am Your daughter. Lead me on Your path of life, and teach me to obey You.

I ask this in the name of Your Son, Jesus. Amen.

DAY 12

TRUSTING GOD
WITH YOUR FUTURE

Tricia

> He gives me new strength.
> He guides me in the right paths,
>   as he has promised.

Psalm 23:3, GNT

I've heard that no creature is more ready to head off and get lost than a sheep. But unfortunately, sheep are also the most likely not to be able to find their way back. I can relate. I headed off in my own direction the first time a handsome teen guy paid attention to me. With a skip and jump, I left the path of waiting and praying for the husband God had for me.

Sometimes sheep wander off because they want to inspect something interesting. Even more commonly, they wander off because they're scared of something they sensed. Have you found yourself doing the same?

I was afraid I would be alone. Other teens were pairing up, and I didn't want to be left out. I also sensed I wasn't worthy, and the attention of a guy would prove I was. In my wandering, I found myself pregnant by a guy who then decided he didn't want to be part of my life. By allowing fears to rule my mind, I found myself in a dark, lonely place I never expected to be.

The good news is what I was looking for wasn't found in a certain direction. It was found in a certain Person. In John 14:6, Jesus said, "I am the way, the truth, and the life." So to get on the right path again, I simply had to call out to Jesus. If you ever find yourself lost or heading down the wrong path, all you have to do is let Jesus know you need His help.

When you cry out in surrender, Father God shows up and shows off. He'll keep His promises because He loves you and because He's trustworthy.

After I turned to God in prayer, He removed those fears from my mind and led me to a husband who loved my son and me unconditionally. Yes, like a sheep, I'd been quick to head off in the wrong direction. But like a wonderful shepherd, Father God was quick to lead me to the right path when I called out to Him.

We all tend to wander off when we're scared of something. In what ways can you turn those fearful thoughts over to God before you get off the right path?

Father,

You know that I'm often scared and quick to allow fears to cloud my thoughts. Please show me that the thoughts that bring fear aren't from You. More than that, they cause me to head in the wrong direction.

At this moment, I call out to You in my wandering. I don't need to find more answers. Instead, I need to trust that You are the answer and that when I walk side by side with You, I will be headed in the right direction. Clear my mind from every fear that has led me astray. I know that You will fulfill Your promises to me because You love me. I believe that Your plans for my future husband and me are trustworthy.

I ask this in the name of Your Son, Jesus. Amen.

*Lord, grant us eyes to see
and ears to hear,
And souls to love and minds
to understand.*

—CHRISTINA ROSSETTI

DAY 13

GETTING RID OF
THINKING ERRORS

Robin

> Stop lying to each other; tell the truth, for we are parts
> of each other and when we lie to each other we are
> hurting ourselves.
>
> *Ephesians 4:25,* TLB

Thinking errors are lies we repeat until we believe them. They mess with our heads and alter our lives. I saw this when I was on the set of a Hallmark Christmas movie that was being made from one of my books. During a break, I asked one of the actors whether he had always wanted to become an actor.

"Yes, but I didn't pursue it seriously until a few years ago."

"Why? What held you back?"

"I was a flop in a high school play, and the teacher said I didn't have what it took to be an actor. I believed him."

"What changed?" I asked. "How did you end up getting cast in movies?"

"A close friend told me I had a thinking error about my acting ability. She said I might be believing a lie, so I needed to erase the old messages and start fresh so I could discover the truth."

Imagine the changes that could happen in your life if you did the same thing. We all know what it's like to be criticized and to think about other people's opinions of us more than we should.

Have you repeated any of these lies to yourself this week?

- *No guy would ever find me attractive or want to be with me.*
- *I failed at my last serious relationship. If I open my heart, I'll get hurt and fail again.*
- *I'm too _____, and that makes me _____.*

It's time to erase the old messages and bravely start fresh in your thinking so that you can discover the truth. When you do, you'll be in a healthy place to make changes where needed. You'll also find that you can hear what God is saying about you more easily.

Attacks on our thinking go back to the Garden of Eden. When the enemy came to Eve, his message was that she was missing out because God was keeping something from her. As soon as she took in that message, the lie settled into her thinking, and that thinking error led to actions that altered everything.

The Lord God came to Adam and Eve in that mess, and as the Relentless Lover, He continues to come to each of us in the middle of our hurts and mistakes. His Spirit quietly pursues a deeper relationship with us.

One of the questions God asked Adam and Eve was "Who told

you that you were naked?" (Genesis 3:11). God had blessed them with innocence, and until the lie came, they believed the truth—that they were complete just the way He made them. It was the enemy who told them they were missing something.

God wants to replace your thinking errors with His truth so that you can believe that you are complete in Him.

What lies about yourself do you keep repeating, and where did those lies come from?

Father God,

Thank You for making me, and thank You for pursuing me. I can see that I have believed lies about who I am and about my value. I want to see myself the way You see me.

Please remove all the damaging comments I've kept in my thinking. Speak truth over my life. Prevent the evil one from speaking lies to me or planting doubts in my mind. Fill me with Your love so that I will stop hurting myself and others by listening to lies.

In Jesus's name, amen.

Search me, O God, and know my heart; test my thoughts. Point out anything you find in me that makes you sad, and lead me along the path of everlasting life.

—PSALM 139:23–24, TLB

DAY 14

CALLING TO GOD IN TEMPTATION

Tricia

As for me, I am poor and needy;
    please hurry to my aid, O God.
You are my helper and my savior;
    O Lord, do not delay.

Psalm 70:5

The first day of any sports practice finds participants falling into two groups: those who are unsure, fearful, and holding back and those who are eager, confident, and ready to show the coach what they can do. Yet the truth is, the enthusiastic athletes need as much coaching as the scared ones. In both cases, participants must understand their need for help. Only when they pause and ask the coach will they receive the support they need.

When it comes to romantic relationships, we also find that young women tend to fall into two categories. First, there are those who are afraid of making mistakes. They fear even building a friendship with a guy, much less starting a dating relationship.

Second, there are those who rush in. They are sure this relationship will play out just like they have seen in the movies. The emotions are intense, and things feel right. How could anything go wrong? Yet in a hurry to reach "happily ever after," these women often miss warning signs along the way. More than that, they forget that they can turn to others for advice.

All of us forget at times that God, too, is available to help. Instead, we believe every decision is up to us, so we don't turn to Him.

No matter whether you're afraid to talk to a guy or you've found yourself caught up in a rush of emotions—and possibly physical intimacy—know that God can help you. He can even save you when you need it. From the moment you whisper His name, God is present and available. He can calm emotions, provide wisdom, and aid you in every temptation.

Whether you're unsure and fearful or eager and confident, God is only a whispered prayer away. All of us need God's help day by day. We just have to be willing to call out to Him. He is quick to provide.

What three temptations do you need to go to God for help with?

Father,

I am thankful that You are my Helper and Savior. Please remind me that I don't have to make decisions or face challenges alone. Forgive me for all the times I've rushed ahead without turning to You first. Also, forgive me for all the times fear has made it impossible for me to take a step in any direction—even the right direction. Soften my heart, and help me understand my need for guidance.

I ask that You don't delay in coming to my aid when I call to You.

In the name of Your Son, Jesus. Amen.

DAY 15

UNDERSTANDING WHAT YOU NEED

Robin

> God, who is your Father, knows your needs before
> you ask him.
>
> *Matthew 6:8, PHILLIPS*

A few years ago, I hosted a group study with eight college-age women. We met once a week and went through the first book Tricia and I co-authored, *Praying for Your Future Husband*. One of the girls, Kara, got a lively discussion going when she described the kind of man she wanted to marry. She knew what she wanted and even had a list, which she read to us.

Another girl said, "It sounds like you want to marry a male version of yourself."

At first, Kara laughed. Then she looked at the list. "You're right. Does that make me a narcissist?"

"No! You're not," the other girls chimed in.

One said, "I think you need someone who is different from you. Opposites attract, right?"

Another added, "Don't you think relationships work better when you're with someone who is strong where you're weak? Someone who challenges you and has a different personality type?"

Kara wasn't sure. "All I know is that I need someone who will be my best friend. We should like the same things, shouldn't we?" She looked at me. "Isn't your husband your best friend?"

The girls were surprised when my immediate answer was "No."

"He is much more than a best friend," I said. "He's my favorite person. I prefer him over any other human. We're opposites in many ways, but he is exactly what I need."

"How did you know what you needed in a husband?"

"To be honest, when I was in college, I thought I knew what I needed. I even was engaged to someone else. But that guy realized before I did that we weren't right together. He walked away and broke my heart."

The girls were quiet.

"What did you do?" Kara asked.

"I cried—a lot. Then I waited to see what God would do. The first thing He did was show me how deeply empathetic I had become toward other women who had had their hearts broken. Then I asked God to show me what He wanted for my life, because I believed He knew what I needed."

I had the girls turn to Matthew 6:8 in their Bibles, and most of them underlined it. I asked whether they believed what Jesus said to His disciples more than two thousand years ago. Does our heavenly Father know what we need before we even ask Him?

That night, most of the girls changed their perspective on what they were looking for in what they started to call "my future favorite person."

Five years later, Kara sent me a text with a beautiful picture from her wedding. I smiled as I read her words: "He's exactly what I needed. God knew."

We can make all kinds of lists and set goals or deadlines based on what we think is best for us. But the truth is, God already knows. All we have to do is ask Him. That's what happens when we pray. We ask. Simply ask. Even if the future doesn't include a husband—or if we have to wait much longer for a spouse than we ever wanted to— He still wants us to ask Him what it is that we need.

If you believe that God knows what you need, what's keeping you from asking Him to make it clear to you?

Dear Father,

You love me. I believe that. I also believe that You know me better than I will ever know myself. Your Son said that You know what I need. Sometimes I have a pretty good idea of what I want. But I don't always know what I need. You do.

Lord, will You reveal to me what I need so that I can be in harmony with You? I surrender to You all the thoughts that have filled my mind on what I need in a husband. Show me what's best for me.

I trust You more than I trust my whims and wishes. You have a good plan for my life.

Thank You. Amen.

DAY 16

HAVING AN ALERT MIND

Tricia

> Pray in the Spirit at all times and on every occasion.
> Stay alert and be persistent in your prayers for all
> believers everywhere.
>
> *Ephesians 6:18*

Travel is one of my favorite activities, and I've been to more than a dozen countries. Usually some ordinary locale on each trip especially captures my heart because I'm watching people go about their everyday lives there.

Sometimes I pause as I'm going about my own life and think about those places. *Right now, someone is walking over the cobblestones on the Charles Bridge in Prague. Someone is sitting in that café in Paris or that coffeehouse in London, enjoying a conversation with a friend. Someone is experiencing a safari in Kenya for the first time, gazing on a sea of zebras.*

The idea that people are experiencing ordinary or extraordinary moments around the world reminds me to pray for others. The same can happen when you're praying for your future husband. On a sunny day, you can imagine him at his summer job or at the lake with friends. On Sunday, you can picture him at church. Or you can picture him pondering the questions he might have about following God. During the holidays, you can imagine family gatherings, and you can pray for his family members too. On every occasion, know that he is probably doing something similar. Both ordinary and exciting moments can remind you to pray.

Maybe you've been expecting to start praying for your future spouse after the two of you meet. But truthfully, everything he faces now will affect him later. You can pray for his health, his faith, his relationships, and his choices, even before you see his face. The more alert and persistent you are, the more protection he will have now over his mind and heart. You can pray even in the middle of ordinary days, yet your prayers can have a tremendous impact. Keeping your mind alert to pray at any moment can dynamically affect your future husband—and your future together.

What are two ordinary events in your life that can trigger you to pray?

Father God,

    Sometimes it's hard to believe that, even now, my future husband is out there going through many of the same types of experiences that I am. Please show me how to use everyday moments to remind me to pray for him.

    Forgive me for the way I've yearned for certain qualities in him without praying for the moments that are molding him into who he will be. Help me fix my mind on effective prayers for him and me. Prayer changes things. Help my prayers change me and support my future husband, even on ordinary days.

    In Your Son's name, amen.

Love the life of your mind,

Furnishing it ever with new thought

So that your countenance glows

With the joy of being alive.

—JOHN O'DONOHUE,
"At the Threshold of Manhood"

DAY 17

RENEWING YOUR MIND

Robin

> Don't copy the behavior and customs of this world,
> but let God transform you into a new person by
> changing the way you think. Then you will learn to
> know God's will for you, which is good and pleasing
> and perfect.
>
> *Romans 12:2*

Romans 12:2 explains one of the most challenging as well as most important processes in our lives. We have to let God transform us into new people. Becoming new doesn't happen automatically after we give our lives to Christ. The pressure to go along with the flow of culture will never let up. The influence of others is often so subtle we don't realize that outside voices have caused us to slide away from God and toward the lies of the evil one.

Several years ago, I saw this happening with some teen girls from

our church that I met with weekly. One of them added a new ex-
clamatory word to her vocabulary. Another girl called her on it,
and the girl responded that the word was only "mild cussing" and
wasn't that bad. Other girls added the word to their conversations.
Soon more aggressive swear words were added, and the girls automatically apologized to me every time they said them in my home.
They seemed to think it was okay to talk like that when they were
around one another, but they knew they should alter their language
when I was there.

Then, at a gathering at my house, one of the girls described a
movie she had seen. I was in the kitchen, but I could hear as she
went into detail about a scene that depicted sex in ways that were
outside societal norms. I stepped into the room and stopped her
mid-sentence. I told her that what she was describing was demean-
ing to the woman and that it wasn't a movie she should have seen.
It didn't model the kind of love and sexual expression God has designed for a man and a woman.

All the girls stared at me. Some seemed to agree. Others nar-
rowed their eyes as if I were out of touch with the kinds of images
they were exposed to every day. Still others were in shock; their
innocent minds had never imagined what had just been described to
them. My heart felt like it was being smothered.

"It's not that bad," one of the girls said. "I've seen worse. My
sister and I watch stuff like that when my parents aren't home. Not
a lot. We mostly watch good things. But I don't think a little dirty
stuff like that sprinkled in with all the good stuff is going to hurt
you. It's the real world."

I paused, thinking of the best way to respond. Then the oven
timer chimed, and I returned to the kitchen and placed the warm
chocolate chip cookies on two plates. Seeing the potted plant on
my windowsill, I took a handful of dirt and sprinkled it over the

cookies on one of the plates. Then I headed back to the living room and put the plates in front of my guests.

"Do these have chocolate powder on top?" the movie reviewer asked with a cookie in her hand.

"No," I answered.

"What is it?"

"Dirt."

"Dirt?" She sniffed it while the others held their cookies and waited.

"It's just 'mild dirt,'" I said, choosing to use the same words one of the girls had employed earlier. "So it isn't that bad. I put only good things into the cookies, so I don't think a little dirt sprinkled over them is going to hurt you."

They all got the point. The cookies on the other plate disappeared quickly. The ones with the dirt were left alone in their "real world" condition.

I loved our discussion that day. I told them that if they wanted to know God's will for their lives, like they said they did, then Romans 12:2 made it clear that they had to stop copying the behavior of the world around them and let God transform them into new people by changing the way they thought.

In what ways can you see that "dirt" has been sprinkled over your thoughts, and in what areas do you need to stop copying the world's behavior?

Dear Heavenly Father,

Forgive me for letting sin slip into my thoughts, my words, and my opinions of what is right and wrong. Remove the dirt from my thoughts. I want You to transform me into a new person. I want You to change the choices I make.

Help me stop imitating others who are not honoring You with their words and actions. Set me apart so that I will not be slowly pulled in.

Please reveal Your truth to me through Your Word, the Bible. I want to experience everything You desire for me and not be easily swayed. I want to know what Your will is for my life. I want to live a life overflowing with all that is good, true, and honoring to You.

In the name of Your Son, amen.

DAY 18

BEING CONTENT

Tricia

> Not that I was ever in need, for I have learned how to
> be content with whatever I have.
>
> *Philippians 4:11*

Five years ago, my husband and I adopted a sibling group of four girls from foster care. Foster care has many difficult aspects, but for some children one good part is Christmas. Churches and organizations purchase Christmas gifts for kids who are in foster care. That meant these four sisters received all the items on their Christmas lists, including clothes, electronics, and toys.

When we adopted them, the girls became part of our family of twelve. With ten children, John and I couldn't afford numerous expensive gifts, but our newly adopted girls didn't understand. I can still remember how crushed I felt when one of our daughters looked at her small pile of presents and said, "Is that all?" I had given what I could but knew it wasn't enough.

You likely have your own long wish list when thinking about what your future husband will be like—and maybe an ideal timeline for when he will show up. In this and other areas of life, our often-unrealistic expectations leave us unsettled and discontent. Life doesn't always go the way we plan. Maybe none of the guys you know meet your standards. It's important to remember that your future husband may still be maturing into the person God is preparing for you. You're still growing too. Or it's possible that marriage isn't on God's list for you.

The thing about contentment is that it comes from the inside, not from a set of circumstances that line up the way we want them to. When we're discontent, we're telling God, "You haven't done enough for me."

Contentment starts in our minds. It's determining to be grateful for what God is preparing for us in a future we can't picture.

Only when our minds are fixed on gratitude will contentment settle into our hearts. Instead of looking around and seeing what we don't have, we can look at the gifts we've been given and be thankful.

What are some things that you have been discontent about, and how can your thoughts change so that you can be grateful for them instead?

Father God,

It's easy to focus on what I don't have at this moment rather than all the good gifts I've been given. Could You please help me trust that You have good plans for me? Help me know that You are my greatest gift.

May I grow closer to You even as I wait. Whenever I start feeling discontent, help me turn my thoughts to You. Also, Lord, gently grow me into the loving, caring, and godly person who will be prepared for all that You have for me.

I ask this in the name of Your Son, Jesus. Amen.

DAY 19

TIME TO DETOX

Robin

> My brothers and sisters, always think about what
> is true. Think about what is noble, right and pure.
> Think about what is lovely and worthy of respect. If
> anything is excellent or worthy of praise, think about
> those kinds of things.
>
> *Philippians 4:8, NIRV*

Have you noticed how your life can be going along nicely and then you find yourself plunged into a muddy emotional pit that swallows all your hope? A big event might push you into the pit—a great loss, a painful injury, an unjust betrayal. Something that derails your attitude and emotional state.

Other stuff can surprise you with how much it hurts. Like finding out that a guy you could be interested in might be interested in you, only to find out he's not. It's way more depressing than it should be because, honestly, you hadn't even decided whether you liked him! But you've slumped. The lie rolls around in your head that you're nobody and no one is ever going to be interested in you.

We have to detoxify if we want to recover from the emotional pain that leaves us hurt and sluggish. Start by telling yourself the truth. The whole truth. As the verse above reminds us, think about what is true. Add to your thoughts those things that are noble, right, and pure. Keep thinking about what is lovely and worthy of respect. Mentally run through all the things that are excellent and worthy of praise.

I have a close friend who went into a downward spin after a huge disappointment. She said she felt as if the foundation of her faith had been shaken. I spent a long weekend with her, and an idea came to me as we sat on the couch talking and crying together.

Every time she voiced a pain-filled thought about what had happened to her, I asked her to tell me one thing she knew was true about God. The first verse that came to her was Romans 8:28: "God causes all things to work together for good" (NASB). I wrote out that verse on a piece of paper, and we went on to the next deep hurt, which she was able to identify as betrayal. Her voice softened as she said, "Jesus will never fail me or abandon me." I looked up Hebrews 13:5 and wrote out that verse. And on we went with the rest of the soul wounds that had punctured her so cruelly, addressing each one with the antidote of God's truth.

My friend loves God. She has His Word in her heart. Over the next few days, we kept going back to the verses I'd written out, and as we did, her countenance changed. She said she was rebuilding her foundation. She wasn't slogging around in depression any longer. Even though her dearest hopes had been shattered, she was back on solid ground and able to dream again, hope again, and, most important, trust God again. We also ate a lot of chocolate, and we had some outrageous laughing fits. I think that helped too.

Always remember: In our hurts big and small, God's Word is the purifying remedy that heals us. The enemy is a liar. Always. Whatever he tells you isn't true. Cleanse your thoughts, and meditate on what the Lover of Your Soul has said to you in His love letter, the Bible.

What lies have pulled you down and kept your thoughts in a place of hurt and depression, and what verses can wash your thoughts with God's truth?

Father God,

I need You. I need Your Word to wash my thoughts and purify my mind. Please remove from my thinking all the lies the enemy has planted in my head. Deliver me from evil.

Restore my soul, Lord. Teach me Your truths. Put Your right thoughts in my mind. Remind me every day that You are at work in my life. Nothing can keep me from You. Nothing can ruin my life. You deliver me, You restore my hopes and dreams, and You heal me.

Please rebuild all the places in my thoughts that have been shattered by hurts and losses, and fill those dark places now with Your light, love, and peace.

I ask this in Jesus's name. Amen.

DAY 20

FORGIVING YOURSELF

Tricia

We are made right with God by placing our faith in
Jesus Christ. And this is true for everyone who
believes, no matter who we are.

For everyone has sinned; we all fall short of God's
glorious standard.

Romans 3:22–23

Recently I pulled my high school cheerleading uniform out of my
closet. I wore it thirty years ago, and it's out of style and about five
sizes too small! Sometimes I think of myself as still being that size.
When I go shopping, I end up trying on things that don't look good
on my current body shape. Since I really see myself only a few
times a day when I look in the mirror, I often forget how much I've
rounded out.

Many of us struggle with accurate perceptions of ourselves. We think we're one way, when actually we're different. Sometimes that misaligned appraisal can bring us a lot of unnecessary pain. (Even more pain than realizing I can't pull off skinny jeans!)

After I married John, I still struggled with the choices I'd made in my past. My mind would replay how much I'd messed up, and those memories were heavy burdens. Even though God had given me a new heart, I had a hard time forgetting the way I'd acted and the choices I'd made.

All that changed when I went to a Bible study where I was reminded that God forgave all my sins—small and big. Even though I'd made wrong choices, God no longer judged me for them. I didn't need to continually judge myself now either. By holding on to shame, I was telling God, "Yes, I know You died for my sins, but what You did wasn't enough." As Micah 7:19 says, "Once again you will have compassion on us. You will trample our sins under your feet and throw them into the depths of the ocean!"

When I dared to trust that God's forgiveness was enough, I opened up my heart to forgiving myself. And whenever my mind tried to replay the choices I'd made, I instead turned those thoughts toward pondering God's goodness to me. I reminded myself that God had forgiven and forgotten the past and that He was focused on the good future He had for me.

The same is true for you. Regardless of what decisions you've made, God's forgiveness will cover your choices. Don't continue to judge yourself or tell yourself how much you've messed up. Instead, open your heart to receive the good things He has prepared for your future. Take time to really think about that.

What sins do you know you need to turn over to God yet feel are too big for Him to forgive?

Father God,

I'm so thankful for Your sacrifice, which has made it possible for me to be forgiven for all my sins.

Lord, just as You have forgiven me, please lift the burdens of pain and shame from my heart. Help me see my sins trampled and thrown into the depths of the sea. I know that to give my whole heart to my future husband, I need to allow You to bring healing to me.

Lord, let Your love rush in. I know it's only when I'm able to accept Your love that I'll be able to accept the love of others. I thank You, God, for the healing You will start and the healing You will continue to do.

I ask this in the name of Your Son, Jesus. Amen.

When we forgive, we set a prisoner free and discover that the prisoner we set free is us.

—LEWIS B. SMEDES,
The Art of Forgiving

Section THREE

HANDS

From Robin

We like to fix things, don't we? We are "hands-on" as humans. Let's be honest: It feels good when we have control.

We hold on to what we value. We also like to stretch out our hands to share what we have with others.

Tricia and I put the "Hands" section last because it's easy to start doing things to feel as if we're moving our lives along. It's more difficult to slow down long enough to dive deep into the core of our feelings and thoughts.

Yet once your heart is uncluttered and at peace and your head is refreshed with clear thinking, there is power in what you put your hands forward to do. Your efforts aren't wasted.

This section can help you recognize the ways in which you are uniquely gifted. You might be holding unexplored potential in your hands. How wonderful it would be if, as you go through this section, you recognize an abandoned ability or find that you can now identify what the next steps should be in a certain area of your life.

Before you begin reading and interacting with the questions and prayers in this section, try doing this: Open both your hands, palms up. Close your eyes and tell God you're available. While you're talking to God with your hands open, you're in the ideal position to release anything you need to let go of. You're also in the perfect posture to expectantly receive whatever God has for you.

If you're going through this book with a small group, this would be a great time to pause and pray for one another. You might even join hands to do so.

From Tricia

When I was a teenager, my bedroom was a huge mess. With school, cheerleading, and guys, I was never home long enough to straighten up the place. I would throw things here and there until every part of the room contained clutter. Can you relate?

As my teen life demonstrates, we often try to fix ourselves by doing more, but that seldom works out well. Robin and I have discovered that the more we allow God to change our hearts and minds, the more our actions will change—for the better. Each step builds on the one before.

We can't wait to see how your life will change as you hand over to our wonderful God everything that you are and hope to become, including your hope of becoming a wife.

DAY 21

THE WORK OF YOUR HANDS

Robin

> Let the favor of the Lord our God be upon us,
>> and establish the work of our hands upon us;
>> yes, establish the work of our hands!
>
> *Psalm 90:17, ESV*

Let's dream about *you*—about what you're drawn to and what you love doing. What is the work of your hands that you've seen God bless? What are the things you've done that other people have complimented or asked for more of? Dream about what it would be like to give more of your time and attention to that talent in the future.

It might well be worth the effort to set aside time to ponder and take notes on what you're good at doing. List your accomplishments that have been praised. Write down things you do that give you joy. Make a note of the kind of work you can stay at for hours, the kind that doesn't feel like work.

Then dream about what it would be like to concentrate more

time and effort on the items you've listed. What do you need in order to make that happen? More training or education? More time in your schedule? A place where you can let the work of your hands take root and grow?

After attending my first writers' conference, I sat down with my journal and gleaned from the random notes I had taken during the keynote sessions and the workshops. I also had jotted down helpful advice from other writers and editors I met at the retreat. It was all a jumble and needed to be re-entered in my journal. I had all the directions, but they had to be organized before I could begin the journey of writing. I needed to prioritize the emerging to-do list.

The first action point soon became clear: location, location, location. Our little rental house was small. Where was I going to set up a work space? The downstairs was an open concept before that was even a thing. I claimed a small space in front of a window and scooted the kitchen table over to make room. I brought in a folding table, moved a chair from the kitchen table, emptied several pens from my purse into a coffee mug, and stacked my writing notebooks in the corner. Ta-da! My work space was ready.

I told a friend what I had done, and she gave me an electric typewriter. Such a generous gift! In a single day, I went from just thinking about writing to setting myself up to become a writer. I had my own space and the necessary equipment. Over the next few years, many articles and books were written in that dedicated spot. When I sat in front of that window, I ignored the phone and the buzzing of the dryer. My back was to the dishes in the sink and the stack of mail on the counter. I was at work, and the favor of the Lord was upon me.

It takes a prayer, a plan, and a first step for the Lord to bless and establish the work of your hands. Start dreaming about what you can do. Take inventory of what you already possess. Prioritize your to-do list and start your journey.

I'm passionate about this process. It may well be part of your path to meeting your future husband. I wish I'd saved all the notes I've received from women who met their spouses while they were in the midst of expanding the work of their hands.

One friend reluctantly agreed to go to a writers' conference, and she met her husband there. Another woman started organizing outings for the singles group at church and married a man who came to the first event. I heard from a girl in her twenties saying that my books motivated her to stop trolling dating sites and go back to school. Yep. There he was in her evening class. Another reader told me that my memoir had inspired her to move to another state because she believed the Lord was asking her to care for her aging mom. She's now married to a man she met through her mom's doctor.

Set aside dreams of your future husband for a while. Dream about what is next for you. Ask God to lead you in developing the abilities, interests, and gifts He's given you, and I believe the favor of the Lord will rest upon you in ways you never would have imagined.

How can you nudge yourself to evaluate your many options for the future and start moving forward?

Dear Author and Finisher of my faith,

I want to focus on what You are asking me to do with this life You've given me. I want to honor You with the work of my hands. Am I in the right place right now? Is this how I should be spending my free time? Is this where I should be working? Is this the best place for me to be living? Should I go to school or hang out with different people?

I want You to write the story of my life because I know that Your plot will be much better than any plot I could come up with. I want to leave all the writing to You. Show me. Lead me. If it's time to start a new chapter, I'm ready. As You reveal the next steps, give me the courage to do whatever You ask of me.

Prepare me, Lord. I want Your favor to rest upon me. I want You to establish the work of my hands.

In Jesus's name, amen.

DAY 22

STRIVING FOR
THE ULTIMATE PRIZE

Tricia

> Do you not know that in a race all the runners run,
> but only one gets the prize? Run in such a way as to
> get the prize. Everyone who competes in the games
> goes into strict training. They do it to get a crown that
> will not last, but we do it to get a crown that will last
> forever.
>
> *1 Corinthians 9:24–25, NIV*

What goals do you have for your future? Not only is having goals important, but so is working toward them. Yet sometimes our "hands-on" efforts disappoint when we reach our goal only to discover that we were working toward the wrong thing.

It's a pretty safe guess that you've seen the Olympics at least a few times. Some people love to watch as much as possible. During my childhood, I was one of those people. I still enjoy it today, and I celebrate when a dedicated athlete wins a medal. Overnight they become a household name, and soon their face shows up on a cereal box.

When Paul wrote to the Corinthians, they had a similar event called the Isthmian Games. They took place on the isthmus—a narrow strip of land with sea on both sides—near Corinth. For the Greek people, winning these games was the greatest honor imaginable. The winners were crowned with garlands of pine, and they returned to their cities as heroes. Their names would be recorded and remembered, and great poets would write about their wins. Speaking to this audience, Paul used their great event to share the truth about a different sort of goal with an even more wonderful grand prize: the eternal crown that comes from standing firm in Jesus Christ.

We need to apply this idea of seeking an ultimate prize to anything we pursue on earth, including the goal of finding a godly husband. Yes, it's important to pray for your future husband. But you also need to prepare yourself for Jesus. A godly marriage isn't the ultimate goal. Knowing Jesus is.

When you set your eyes on Jesus and run toward Him, you are also moving toward the man God has planned for you. How do I know? Because the right man will be moving toward God too.

When we run toward God, He gives us what our hearts desire, namely Himself. Yet He gives us even more. In your pursuit of what is best, Jesus will also bring good to you. Trust Him for that.

What is one habit you can develop to help you in your pursuit of knowing Jesus better?

Father God,

It's easy for me to become distracted by all the good things I could pursue. I know it's not wrong to seek after many of these things, such as my future husband. Yet I know that my greater goal needs to be seeking after You.

Lord, I pray that You will become the focus of my heart. Help me trust that everything else will fall into place when I run after You. I pray that I will not grow weary in my pursuit of knowing You better and loving You more. Help me, Lord, to develop positive habits and to stay strong.

I ask this in the name of Your Son, Jesus. Amen.

DAY 23

HOLDING HANDS

Robin

I am holding you by your right hand—I, the Lord
your God—and I say to you, Don't be afraid; I am here
to help you.

Isaiah 41:13, TLB

This may sound silly, but when I was eleven, I wanted a certain boy
at school to walk me home and hold my hand. Holding hands was
the most romantic expression of love and affection I could imagine.
I thought about holding hands with him all the time. I even wrote
a poem about how it would feel, walking hand in hand under the
jacaranda trees that lined the street where I lived.

Disaster struck when I hinted at my fairy-tale wish to my friend
and she told the boy! The next day I found a note on my desk. He
had drawn an ugly picture of a face covered with zits and written
my name underneath. The next day the note was a frog with my

name. He left four more notes, each one grosser than the one before.

I never told anyone about the bullying. But I was afraid all the
time. I didn't want to go to school. I didn't want to be around any
of the kids in my class because I feared they all knew about his hate
notes. I destroyed the notes along with my dream of any guy ever
liking me or wanting to hold my hand as we walked home.

The summer I turned twelve, I went to church camp, and on the
last night, I gave my heart to the Lord. I surrendered my whole life
to Him.

I was given an easy-to-understand Bible, and as I read it, I began
to think of Jesus as the One who truly loved me and always would.
Just as it says in Isaiah 41:13, God is the One who holds my hand.
He will always be with me, and He is walking me all the way home
to heaven.

I've never grown tired of this mental image of my walk through
life with the Lord. The older I become, the more I see that this
image of holding hands reflects what the Lord desires our relationship to be like. He wants us to be that close—side by side, hand in
hand, fingers intertwined.

The image of holding hands always comes to mind when I fold
my hands to pray. It reminds me not to be afraid of what anyone
may say or do to me. I am with Jesus. He is with me. He wants to
be with me. He wants to help me, and He wants me always to stay
close to Him, holding on to His nail-pierced hand.

What image comes to mind when you think of Jesus always being beside you?

Dear Prince of Peace,

You are the One who is closer than a brother. You are my friend who loves me at all times. You want to hold me close. You want to hold my hand. Every moment of my life, You are with me.

Lord, I reach out my right hand to You. Grasp it. Hold on to me. Take away all my fears. Help me. Please remove all memories of human rejection. Demolish all the hurts I have experienced. Restore my childlike innocence, and keep me by Your side all the days of my life.

Thank You, Lord. Amen.

We stood hand in hand,
like two children, and there
was peace in our hearts
for all the dark things
that surrounded us.

—SIR ARTHUR CONAN DOYLE,
The Sign of the Four

DAY 24

GROWING IN MATURITY

Tricia.

> When I was a child, I spoke and thought and reasoned as a child. But when I grew up, I put away childish things.
>
> *1 Corinthians 13:11*

In sixth grade, I wanted a boyfriend more than anything. I wanted a guy to talk to on the phone and pass notes to. I wanted someone to think I was pretty. I wanted to dance with someone at school dances rather than sit on the bleachers, awkwardly watching.

But when I became an unwed teen mom years later, I grew up overnight. Playing the "Does he like me?" or "Am I good enough?" game no longer interested me. Instead, I seriously considered what qualities were important in a future husband.

Maturity in our Christian walk is similar. As a new Christian, I would fit "following God" into what I was already doing. I watched

TV shows that weren't too bad. I attended church and Bible study, but the messages I heard were things to think about, rather than life-transforming truth. My faith was in my head instead of also being in my heart.

But when I worked my way through *Experiencing God* by Henry Blackaby and Claude King in my mid-twenties, I discovered that God desired to be active in my life. I also realized that I didn't have to question what God had in store for my future. Instead, I should look around, see where He was already working in my life, and join Him.

As someone who loved to read novels—and who always thought of story ideas—I decided to pursue becoming a writer. As someone who wanted to encourage young moms who were struggling as I had, I chose to volunteer at a pregnancy care center. Immediately my life changed, and I witnessed God working in amazing ways.

We're being childish when we believe we can turn to God only when it's convenient. Playing the "Does he like me?" or "Am I good enough?" game doesn't benefit a relationship with a guy—or with God. These relationships matter much more than we imagine, and dedication to growth and maturity makes all the difference. Put your hand to the work of growing your relationship with God.

What can you choose to do to become more mature in your Christian walk instead of fitting God into what you're already doing?

Father God,

It breaks my heart to think how often I've pushed You to the side because other things seemed more important. I know that living with childish goals won't get me far in my relationship with You, just as it won't get me far in preparing for my future husband. Help me genuinely consider where I put my attention and to whom I offer my heart.

I desire to grow into someone trustworthy and dedicated to You and my future husband. Protect me from being hurt by childish choices. Lead me to join You, Lord, in the work You are already doing in my life. Help me put away what's no longer necessary so that I am free to live more fully for You.

I ask this in the name of Your Son, Jesus. Amen.

DAY 25

WHAT'S IN YOUR HANDS?

Robin

> Make a careful exploration of who you are and the
> work you have been given, and then sink yourself into
> that.
>
> *Galatians 6:4, MSG*

Close friends see things in us that we can't see. True friends will speak truth into our lives if they observe that we're overlooking our own strengths. Sometimes we ignore what we're good at because it comes easily to us, so we think it's something everyone can do without much effort. Friends notice these strengths and abilities and can affirm the gifts that God has given us.

We lived on Maui for ten years, and I got to know a lot of girls. I led group studies and often met up with young women individually for deep conversations. I found a common theme among these women—they didn't see themselves as special or gifted.

One of them had been working for years at a job that she didn't love, but she was afraid to resign because it was risky to pursue what she really wanted to do. Then the economy shifted, and she was let go from that job.

She came over, and we talked about all the possibilities that were now open to her. She was making a careful exploration of all her options, as the verse above encourages us to do.

With a hug and a prayer, she went back to her apartment and took a brave step by filling out a scholarship application. Within a few months, she was back in school, pursuing the career she desired.

Another young woman started crying one day at my house as we sat outside sipping iced tea. I had been telling her all the abilities I saw in her and asked, "What do you think God is inviting you to do with your unique talents?"

Her reply was that for years she had thought only about who she wanted to spend her life with. She hadn't thought about what she wanted to spend her life *doing*. Her heart was confused because now the person she had longed for was engaged to someone else.

As we talked, I was glad to see that she was ready to let go of her hazy, unfulfilled dreams about the future and to see herself with fresh eyes. All her hope had been tethered to the wrong "him."

"You have so much talent and so many resources right in your lap," I said. To convince her, I listed her strengths and reminded her of things she had excelled in. While I talked, it seemed as if she uncurled her fingers and, for the first time, looked at the riches she already held in her hands.

Over the years, I had the joy of seeing quite a number of those young Maui girls change in stunning ways. Once they chose a new path toward abundant life in Christ, I watched on the sidelines and found it crazy fun to see how all sorts of opportunities and blessings came their way. Some have married, some are seriously dating men who love God, and some are genuinely content to be in a season of life during which they can fully pursue their giftings and interests.

For the young woman who sat on the lanai with me and wept, once she shifted her focus from the "who"—the man who never returned her interest—to the "what" God had prepared for her, options opened up that she probably wouldn't have seen before.

The last time I talked with her, I couldn't help but notice how attractive she had become. Her faith is blooming beautifully. Her life is full, and her countenance is open and glowing. I found myself thinking she had become irresistible.

What close and trusted friend can you ask to hold up a mirror and help you "make a careful exploration of who you are and the work you have been given"?

Father God,

Open my eyes so I can see who You made me to be. Open my hands so I can recognize the gifts You've given to me. Open my heart so I can hear You as You lead me into what's next for my life.

Lord, if I've been focusing on a guy or longing for a husband rather than looking to You, please take my eyes off that hope and fix them on You and Your purpose for me. I want to radiate Your love and be content in the work You've created me to do. I believe that You will lead me. Please put a close friend in my life who will help me see the gifts You've given me.

I pray this in the name that is above all names. Amen.

Faith sees the invisible, believes the unbelievable, and receives the impossible.

—Corrie ten Boom,
Jesus Is Victor

DAY 26

FINDING HOME

Tricia

> Christ will make his home in your hearts as you trust
> in him. Your roots will grow down into God's love
> and keep you strong. And may you have the power to
> understand, as all God's people should, how wide, how
> long, how high, and how deep his love is.
>
> *Ephesians 3:17–18*

"Home is where the heart is." Have you heard that saying? My daughter Leslie discovered this to be true when she left our home in the United States to do missionary work in the Czech Republic, which is in central Europe. After allowing Christ to make His home in her heart, she decided to place herself in God's hands and pursue the work that He had called her to do.

At age twenty-one, Leslie left behind her parents, her siblings, her friends, and everything she had known. Because less than 1 percent of people in the Czech Republic consider themselves evangelical Christians and because female missionaries generally outnumber men four to one, Leslie knew that her odds of finding a man who loved God were slim. She surrendered her desire for marriage to God and moved to the mission field anyway, accepting that she would never marry. She decided her relationship with God would be home, no matter where she was.

Not long after Leslie moved to Europe, she met a Czech guy named Honza through a mutual friend. He was a believer but nothing like the future husband Leslie had always imagined—more of a beer-meat-and-potatoes European than the hippie worship pastor she had envisioned. Plus, he didn't feel called to full-time ministry like she was. But over time she began to appreciate the love and care he showed to all around him and how his life complemented hers.

Two years after Leslie moved to the Czech Republic, she married Honza in a beautiful cathedral. Through the years they've learned how to build a multicultural, bilingual, God-loving home.

When it comes to envisioning a future loving home, we need to first allow Christ to make His home in us, and then we need to trust Him for what that home will look like. Then, wherever He leads us, we'll discover the home He had in mind for us all along.

What is one faith step you can take to help you see God as your true home no matter where you are?

Father God,

I want to fully open my heart to You, and I want my heart to be Your home. I also desire to trust You with the home You're preparing for me—in this life and in eternity. Help me believe in Your good plans, Lord, wherever You lead.

I know my efforts at building a home will fail unless I allow You to be my First Love. Lord, I desire to understand how wide, how long, how high, and how deep Your love is. Help me trust You enough to show me.

I ask this in the name of Your Son, Jesus. Amen.

You can give without loving,
but you can never love
without giving. The great
acts of love are done by those
who are habitually performing
small acts of kindness.

—Robert Louis Stevenson

DAY 27

A GIVING HAND

Robin

> She opens her hand to the poor
>   and reaches out her hands to the needy.
>
> *Proverbs 31:20, ESV*

Here's a fun fact: Being generous activates the part of your brain that makes you feel pleasure. When you give, the hormone oxytocin is released. Oxytocin is known to balance emotions. How great is that? You improve your emotional health when you are generous to others.

If you have siblings, think about how often during your childhood you were told to share. Isn't it interesting that giving to others doesn't come naturally to us? Our human nature bends our thoughts in the opposite direction. We tend to take what we want and expect others to give to us. We don't say that aloud, but entitlement is embedded in each of us.

My sister and I often bickered over chores. We became kinder to each other as we matured, but in my early teen years, I got mad if I had to do something as simple as loading the dishwasher when it wasn't my turn. Selfishness was at the root of much of the slow-burning anger I held on to during those years. I felt that I was being robbed of my time and freedom to choose what I wanted to do. My stubborn attitude released all the other kinds of hormones—not emotion-balancing oxytocin.

I remember coming across Hebrews 10:24 when I was a teen-ager, and I often went back to it: "In response to all he has done for us, let us outdo each other in being helpful and kind to each other and in doing good" (TLB).

Something inside me wanted to learn how to do that—to be helpful and kind instead of offended and angry whenever I felt imposed on. It's an ongoing process, but it starts with generosity.

Over the years, I've spent time with newlywed wives. Most of them have quietly told me, "I didn't think marriage would be this hard. It's the little things that make me mad." The expectation—and yes, I had this too—was that once they were married, their love would propel them to pour out a continuous stream of kindness toward each other. Unlike their experiences with roommates, they would never face days when the other person used the last of the milk or didn't take out the trash. They imagined that, as man and wife, neither of them would ever be that selfish, because they loved each other.

The truth is, we are selfish. All of us. We don't like to think of ourselves that way, do we? We like to think we are kind and generous. We like to give. We want to give. So why aren't we practicing the art of generosity every day in the little things and with the people we live with now?

Giving begins with a decision. We choose to be generous with our time, resources, patience, respect, encouragement, and love. The more we practice giving generously now, the more consistently generous we'll be in the years ahead. It will begin to feel natural to share without expecting anything in return.

Find ways to give generously—make a financial donation, take time to help someone in need, or do something as simple as cheerfully offering to go above and beyond for a person who least expects it.

Your balanced emotions will thank you. In the future, you'll be grateful that you trained your hands to reach out to others in generosity and love.

What is the first thing that came to mind when you read the words "Find ways to give generously," and what would it take for you to follow through and do it?

Gracious Lord,

You have given me everything. You provide all my needs, and You have blessed me many times with the desires of my heart. You are so generous with me, Lord. Thank You.

Forgive me for all the times I have selfishly withheld kindness or any sort of gift. Release me from self-centered thinking, and fill me with compassion and understanding for others. I want to learn how to be a more generous woman. I want to train my hands to reach out and give without expecting anything in return. Fill me with Your love.

In Jesus's name, amen.

DAY 28

LIVING WISELY

Tricia

> Be careful how you live. Don't live like fools, but like
> those who are wise.
>
> *Ephesians 5:15*

The first time my future husband, John, saw me was at church, where his father was the pastor. John was on active duty as a Marine. He had come home for weekend leave, and that Sunday, I was sitting one row behind him with my mom. At that church, the congregants would turn around and greet people before the sermon started. John says he turned around to shake my hand, saw me, and thought I was beautiful. Later, after church, he asked his mom about me.

"Stay away from Tricia. She's trouble," his mom told him. And she was right. I was trouble. I was wrapped up in dating the wrong guys and trying to have as much "fun" as possible. Because I wasn't making positive choices, a good Christian guy didn't need to be spending time with me.

At the time, I didn't understand that my actions had consequences. I didn't realize that by making my own decisions—and pursuing what I wanted—I was taking myself out of God's hands.

Fast-forward a few years, and John saw me again at church. He was out of the military and living in the area. This time, I was praising God during the worship service. I was also eight months pregnant. It was during my pregnancy that I dedicated my life to God. Then, after I had my son, John's mom and my mom got together to play matchmakers—working to set me up with John. Yes, the very pastor's wife who had told her son that I was trouble later worked to bring us together. What had changed? Me. I was a new person, and I was living differently than before. Giving my heart to the Lord had changed me. I chose to follow God and make good choices, and the change was evident to others.

During my pregnancy, I had prayed for a husband, but I also started to live differently. I finally grasped that my actions have consequences, for bad or good. Yes, it's good to pray, but the next step is to make the answers to those prayers possible by following God. How we pray is important, but how we live is equally important.

What types of lifestyle choices do you need to make to line up with what you're praying for?

Father God,

Sometimes I forget that praying for my future husband is just a first step. It's also essential to live the kind of life that will make possible the hoped-for answers to those prayers. Help me live wisely and make positive choices. Remind me that my choices now affect my present and my future. Release me from bad habits that keep me from fully following You.

Lord, as I walk with You, I know You will lead me on the right path. And if I quiet my mind and my heart, You will guide me through the Bible and through Your sweet Holy Spirit within me. May my faithful choices be witnessed by others and point them to saving faith in You.

I ask this in the name of Your Son, Jesus. Amen.

DAY 29

BEING GUIDED BY INTEGRITY

Tricia

> The integrity and moral courage of the
> upright will guide them,
> But the crookedness of the treacherous
> will destroy them.
>
> *Proverbs 11:3, AMP*

A friend of mine, Todd Tilghman, was in a popular reality singing competition. He met some of the most admired musical artists in the world. Yet after his time in Los Angeles, he talked most about the ordinary people he had met. Behind the scenes, he had numerous conversations about God and faith. To my friend, star status mattered less than how open someone was. It turned out that stagehands and producers appreciated being noticed and found joy in the conversations.

In his everyday life, my friend's integrity and moral courage governed the type of music he listened to and the type of people he spent time with. These qualities guided him in Hollywood too. All noticed his care for others, whether famous or not.

It doesn't take much to get offtrack from living a life of integrity. We tell ourselves that it's okay to tell a half-truth so we don't get in trouble. And it's not that bad when we gossip about someone, because everyone does it. Or we argue that we can enjoy popular music while ignoring the lyrics. The problem is that the media we consume soon starts to consume us. Our focus shifts away from God to the things the world considers popular. Soon we find ourselves wrapped up in our favorite TV stars and musical artists (who happen to be called *idols*!), and we spend less and less time focusing on God.

It takes moral courage to choose *not* to focus on what's popular in the world or to mimic the actions of those who don't follow God. When it comes to the media we consume, it's important to ask, "Is this leading me closer to God's ideas or the world's ideas?" When we consider telling a half-truth or gossiping, we can ask, "Is this what a person of integrity would do?"

The closer you draw to God's ideas, allowing yourself to be guided by integrity, the more you're able to offer hope, faith, and wisdom to the world. As a result, you'll become the type of person to whom others will be drawn, including your future husband. And along the way, you'll discover that the straight path is one of joy.

What impact do the actions you're currently taking have on who you are as a person and what you offer to others?

Father God,

Sometimes it's hard to remember that the media I consume affects both my heart and my walk. Instead of conforming to the ways of the world, may I become someone whom the world turns to for advice and support. I desire for my choices to draw me closer to You. I want to walk the straight path, which leads me to You.

May I be wrapped up in You, Lord, more than anything or anyone else. May I be known for my integrity in all things.

I ask this in the name of Your Son, Jesus. Amen.

DAY 30

GOD'S INVISIBLE HAND

Robin

I am trusting you, O LORD,
   saying, "You are my God!"
My future is in your hands.

Psalm 31:14–15

I hope that you have many character-shaping adventures before you get married. I hope that God gives you stretching experiences. Why? Because as a result of those episodes, you will see God's invisible hand, and it will strengthen you and prepare you to be a more understanding and patient friend, wife, co-worker, and mother.

When I was in my twenties, I backpacked around Europe for the summer with some of my girlfriends. We saw the invisible hand of God directing us many times. The most remarkable moment happened in Venice, Italy.

We woke up in our youth hostel bunk beds and heard the rain pouring outside. I mean, buckets of rain. Undaunted and in a hurry, we strapped on our backpacks, pulled up our hoods, and frantically sloshed our way to the train station. We were meeting friends in Florence that afternoon, and back then, we had no cellphones. If we missed the train, there would be no way to let them know we were still coming. We pressed on through puddles and mud and were soaked by the time we could see the station ahead of us. After running the rest of the way, we arrived at our platform just in time to see the caboose of the 7 A.M. train as it left the station, headed to Florence without us.

None of us said a word. We found a table at the coffee bar and ordered cappuccinos. All we could do was try to get dry and wait for the next train, which left in five hours. Our waiter seemed to have forgotten us, and the longer we waited, the grouchier and more miserable we became. In our impatience, we started the worst conversation we had had the whole trip.

Who was in charge of setting the alarm? Why didn't she set it for earlier?

Why did it take a certain one of us so long to get her stuff packed back at the hostel?

We could have made it if one of us, in her impractical shoes, hadn't had trouble keeping up with the rest of us.

We stopped muttering and turned our attention to where a cluster of people had gathered, talking excitedly in Italian. A fellow tourist leaned over and said, "Did you hear? A mudslide took out the tracks. The train to Florence was derailed. They say it fell into a ravine."

Our eyes flashed the shock we felt, followed by expressions of sincere apology to one another for the accusations we had been tossing around. Gratitude replaced our grumbling. The invisible hand of God had made us miss the train. Not a pair of shoes or a backpack or an alarm clock.

We made it to Florence later that day via a different route, and yes, we found our friends. We arrived with our spirits softened and humbled. During our remaining weeks of travel, our patience with one another grew. Our flexibility and trust in God's leading expanded.

"My future is in your hands" (Psalm 31:15). Those six words are such a simple declaration. But what a strong foundation. Say it over and over. When we believe—I mean, really, truly believe at the gut level—that our future is in God's hands, we won't accuse others of messing up our plans. We won't become angry when our schedule must go on hold or when a relationship with a guy is obliterated. We won't wrongfully blame ourselves or others. We will trust God.

My girlfriends and I could have been among the many fatalities or injured passengers that day on the 7 A.M. train, but God's invisible hand was shaping a different plan for us. The three of us all married men who love God, and at some point in our long marriages, all of us served in full-time ministry as couples. The stretching experiences we girlfriends shared during that summer prepared us for the careers we've enjoyed, the men we married, the children we raised, and the many challenges that have filled our lives. All of us would say that God's invisible hand led us all the way.

If you believe that God is really in control, what do you need to start saying to yourself and others to express that your future is in God's hands?

Great Shepherd,

I confess to You, Lord, that I often respond with anger, hurt, and depression when things don't go the way I want them to. Sometimes I can see things so clearly in my mind, and I set up a plan to make everything go the way I want it to.

But I know that ultimately You are in control. You hold my life, my dreams, and my plans in Your hands. I trust You to work out Your plan for my life.

In Jesus's name, amen.

Every experience God gives us, every person He puts in our lives is the perfect preparation for a future that only He can see.

—CORRIE TEN BOOM

A FINAL THOUGHT

Tricia and Robin

Our hearts are so full of love for you. You've been in our prayers as we wrote every page of this book. Our desire has been that the words on these pages encourage you and point you to Jesus. More than anything, our hope is that you will draw close to Him.

Even though our words may be forgotten, Jesus will never fail you. He will lead you and guide you on a beautiful life journey even more wonderful than you can imagine. How do we know? He's done it for us, and every day, we see how He's doing the same for those we know who love Him unconditionally.

That's not to say that life has always been easy. We still live in a fallen world filled with people and problems, sin and loss. Yet when you remain close to Jesus, He will be with you in those situations too. Even when things are hard, Jesus wants to be the One to help you and strengthen you. Remember? It's like a marriage. For better or worse, for richer or poorer, in sickness and in health. Forever. Your relationship with Him is a sacred union, and the deeper you grow in your love for Him, the more abundant and uncomplicated your love for others will become.

Thank you for taking the time to go through these thirty devotions. We hope that you answered the thirty questions thoughtfully and that they helped you assess where you're at right now. And most of all, we hope that you prayed your little heart out at the end of each day's reading. God hears every prayer. He is at work in your life. Know that we are cheering you on. May you be faithful to God and discover His wonderful faithfulness in return!

DISCUSSION QUESTIONS

We all need friends, particularly friends who challenge and encourage us spiritually. Group studies provide a wonderful opportunity to strengthen friendships by diving deeper into discussions about life topics that really matter.

We believe getting your heart, head, and hands in line with what God says about you is a life topic that *really* matters. Especially when you pay attention to those issues *before* you meet your future husband.

Why not gather a few friends—or even just one committed bestie—and use this book to start a meaningful conversation? Or recommend this as a study for your youth group? We've crafted the questions on the following pages to make it easy for you to open up and share in a small group or in one to-one mentoring.

To help you with those conversations, this study guide provides questions and key talking points inspired by each of the book's three sections. We wrap up in our fourth section with our special "What God Says About You" list. As you celebrate God's amazing love for you, each person in the group can share which of these verses means the most to her and why.

As you're going through these questions, sometimes the conversation may drift a bit too far from what's being discussed. If that happens, your group can get back on track by simply asking the next question listed in the guide.

Our desire is that by prayerfully talking through these topics, each of you will draw closer to the Lord and to one another. May you be doubly blessed by going through this book together.

Enjoy!

Section One: Heart

1. Share why you want to do this study. What do you hope to get out of it?

2. Was there a time in your life when you said "I do" to Jesus as Robin described in day 2? Briefly share about that moment.

3. If you were to take your group on a walk through the garden of your heart right now, what would you point out to them? What's growing robustly, and what needs to be weeded out?

4. Jude 2 expresses what it looks like when we choose to trust God. Read the different translations below. What words stand out to you? What needs or concerns in your life do those words speak to right now?

   - The Message reads, "Relax, everything's going to be all right; rest, everything's coming together; open your hearts, love is on the way!"
   - The King James Version reads, "Mercy unto you, and peace, and love, be multiplied."
   - The Amplified Bible reads, "May mercy and peace and love be multiplied to you [filling your heart with the spiritual well-being and serenity experienced by those who walk closely with God]."

5. Have you had any "falling in love" experiences? What have you learned from those relationships?

6. When Tricia wrote about healing from a broken heart (day 5), she said, "God didn't glue together the broken pieces. He gave me a new heart." In what ways is a new heart better than a pieced-together heart? Also, consider the description Robin gave of her home on Maui that was in serious need of renovation (day 8). How has God healed your heart after it's been broken? How have your experiences shaped how you guard your heart?

Section Two: Head

1. How have thinking errors affected your life? If you would like, share a specific thinking error you struggle with.

2. In what ways have you seen your thoughts shifting as you've read this book? In what ways are you choosing to forgive? In what ways are you trusting God more? What has helped you identify the lies you've believed?

3. What's the most problematic old way of thinking you need to let go of? What steps can you take—regardless of how small—to cultivate a healthy, God-focused mind?

4. On day 17, Robin talked about sprinkling a handful of dirt over a plate of cookies. In what parts of your life has "dirt" been sprinkled over something good? What adjustments can you make to move toward making different choices?

5. List any obstacles that keep you from being truly content with your life. Which of these obstacles are within your power to change? Which ones can only God change? Have you asked Him to do so? Your group might want to spend some time praying aloud for one another or silently asking God for His help.

6. On day 19, Robin explained how she asked her friend to think of "one thing she knew was true about God." What's the first

true thing about God that comes to your mind? What verse verifies that what you believe about Him is true? If you need help, try searching an online Bible using the keyword search. Write down the verse(s) you discover.

Section Three: Hands

1. Pause long enough to dream about what's next for you—dreams that don't depend on having a husband. Share some of the possibilities. Or help one another come up with options. What might it look like to pursue one of those dreams?

2. Tricia wrote about growing in maturity (day 24) and quoted 1 Corinthians 13:11: "When I was a child, I spoke and thought and reasoned as a child. But when I grew up, I put away childish things." What childish things do you need to put away?

3. Consider Galatians 6:4: "Make a careful exploration of who you are and the work you have been given" (MSG). Take a few minutes to list your strengths. Sometimes our own gifts are invisible to us because they come naturally. If you need help spotting yours, think about some of your good qualities that others have praised you for. You probably have observed one another's strengths as you've been meeting together. Feel free to point these out. While you discuss your unique gifts and abilities, be sure to talk about how they can honor God and benefit others.

4. On day 25, Robin wrote about her friend: "Once she shifted her focus from the 'who'—the man who never returned her interest—to the 'what' God had prepared for her, options opened up that she probably wouldn't have seen before." When have you needed to make a big shift in your focus? Did you make the shift? What were the results? Or do you need to make a shift now? How would you do that?

5. Corrie ten Boom said, "Faith sees the invisible, believes the un-believable, and receives the impossible." When have you, in faith, done what Corrie talked about? How did you know that God was right there with you? What situation are you in now in which you need to follow Corrie's advice?

6. Get creative, and consider how you can partner together to do what Proverbs 31:20 says: "She opens her hand to the poor and reaches out her hands to the needy" (ESV). Make a plan, set a date, and put your hands to good work by serving others. Enjoy serving together!

Section Four: Wrap-Up

1. When your heart is uncluttered, when your mind is trans-formed, and when your hands are open, your life will change. The best way to continue to live in the freedom of new life is to focus on God's Word and His opinion of you. Read the follow-ing list of Scripture verses in which God expresses the ways He is present in your life.* Choose your favorite promises and share them with one another. Many additional verses declare God's purpose and passion for His children. Feel free to add those to this list. We hope you'll refer back to these verses often as a re-minder of how much you're loved by the One who created you and calls Himself your Bridegroom.

WHAT GOD SAYS ABOUT YOU

You were made in My image. (Genesis 1:27)

You are My treasured possession. (Exodus 19:5)

---

* This list was originally published in *Spoken For: Embracing Who You Are and Whose You Are* by Robin Jones Gunn and Alyssa Joy Bethke.

If you seek Me with your whole heart, you will find Me.
(Deuteronomy 4:29)

When you are brokenhearted, I am close to you.
(Psalm 34:18)

Delight in Me, and I will give you the desires of your heart.
(Psalm 37:4)

I know everything about you. (Psalm 139:1)

I know when you sit down and when you stand up.
(Psalm 139:2)

I am familiar with all your ways. (Psalm 139:3)

I knit you together when you were in your mother's womb.
(Psalm 139:13)

You are fearfully and wonderfully made. (Psalm 139:14)

All your days were written in My book before there was
one of them. (Psalm 139:16)

My thoughts toward you are as countless as the sand on the
seashore. (Psalm 139:17–18)

As a shepherd carries a lamb, I have carried you.
(Isaiah 40:11)

I knew you before you were conceived. (Jeremiah 1:5)

My plans for your future are for good, to give you hope.
(Jeremiah 29:11)

I have loved you with an everlasting love. (Jeremiah 31:3)

I will take pleasure in doing good things for you and will do
those things with all My heart and soul. (Jeremiah 32:41)

I want to show you great and marvelous things.
(Jeremiah 33:3)

I rejoice over you with singing. (Zephaniah 3:17)

I am your provider. I will meet all your needs.
  (Matthew 6:31–33)

I know how to give good gifts to My children.
  (Matthew 7:11)

I gave you the right to become My child when you received
  My Son, Jesus, and believed in His name. (John 1:12)

I have prepared a place for you. I will come back for you
  and take you to Myself so that we can be together forever. (John 14:3)

I love you even as I love My only Son. (John 17:23)

I revealed My love for you through Jesus. (John 17:26)

I determined the exact time of your birth and where you
  would live. (Acts 17:26)

In Me, you live and move and have your being. (Acts 17:28)

I am for you and not against you. (Romans 8:31)

I will never allow anything to separate you from My love.
  (Romans 8:35–39)

I gave My Son so that you and I could be reconciled.
  (2 Corinthians 5:19)

I am your peace. (Ephesians 2:14)

I am able to do more for you than you could possibly imagine. (Ephesians 3:20)

I am at work in you, giving you the desire and the power to
  fulfill My good purpose for you. (Philippians 2:13)

I gave you a spirit not of fear but of power, love, and self-
  control. (2 Timothy 1:7)

Every good gift you receive comes from My hand.
  (James 1:17)

I desire to lavish My love on you because you are My child and I am your Father. (1 John 3:1)

My love for you is not based on your love for Me. (1 John 4:10)

You can know the complete expression of love in Me. (1 John 4:16)

I will dwell with you in the new creation. You will be My people. I will be your God. (Revelation 21:3)

I will one day wipe away every tear from your eyes, and there will be no more crying or pain or sorrow. (Revelation 21:4)

I have written your name in My book. (Revelation 21:27)

I invite you to come. (Revelation 22:17)

2. Finally, share your favorite insight from this book. End by praying together and thanking God for His transforming work in you!

Meet the Authors

Robin Jones Gunn is the award-winning, bestselling author of more than one hundred books and is best known for the timeless Christy Miller series for teen girls. Four of her novels have been adapted into Hallmark Christmas movies. She's a frequent keynote speaker at international and local events. After living on Maui for a decade, Robin and her husband now live in Southern California. You can connect with Robin:

Facebook: www.facebook.com/authorrobinjonesgunn
Instagram: www.instagram.com/robingunn
Twitter: https://twitter.com/robingunn
Website: www.robingunn.com

Tricia Goyer is a speaker, podcast host, and *USA Today* bestselling author of more than eighty books. Tricia writes in numerous genres including fiction, parenting, and marriage for adults as well as books for children and teens. She's a wife and a homeschooling mom of ten children, including seven daughters! She loves to mentor writers through WriteThatBook. Club. Tricia lives near Little Rock, Arkansas. You can connect with Tricia:

Facebook: www.facebook.com/authortriciagoyer
Instagram: www.instagram.com/triciagoyer
Website: www.triciagoyer.com